The Layperson's
Introduction
to the
New Testament

CARL H. MORGAN

The Layperson's Introduction to the New Testament

JUDSON PRESS®   VALLEY FORGE

The Layperson's Introduction to the New Testament

Copyright © 1968, 1991

Judson Press, Valley Forge, PA 19482-0851

Unless otherwise indicated, Bible quotations in this volume are from the Revised Standard Version of the Bible, copyrighted 1946, 1952, © 1971, 1973 by the Division of Christian Education of the National Council of the Churches of Christ in the U.S.A., and used by permission.

Other versions of the Bible quoted in this book are: *The Holy Bible*, King James Version.

Library of Congress Cataloging-in-Publication Data

Morgan, Carl H. (Carl Hamilton), 1901-1983.
     The layperson's introduction to the New Testament / Carl H. Morgan.
        p.   cm.
     Rev. ed. of: The layman's introduction to the New Testament. 1968.
     Includes bibliographical references.
     ISBN 0-8170-1162-5
     1. Bible.—N.T.—Introductions.   I. Morgan, Carl H. (Carl
Hamilton), 1901-1983. Layman's introduction to the New Testament.
II. Title.
BS2330.2.M59   1991
225.6'1—dc20   90-47528
                                                   CIP

The name JUDSON PRESS is registered as a trademark in the U.S. Patent Office.

Printed in the U.S.A.

2004 2005 2006 2007 2008 2009 2010   8 7 6 5

PREFACE

When the decision was made to let *The Layman's Introduction to the New Testament* go out of print, we thought that it was nearing the end of its productive life and would soon be supplanted by newer books; we felt that it had earned an honorable retirement. But requests for the book kept coming. It became apparent that, with its concise overview of the New Testament, its clear exposition of the New Testament's development, and its basic introduction to the elements of biblical criticism, the book met a need. And so, we decided to call it back from retirement and give it a new life as *The Layperson's Introduction to the New Testament.*

Dr. Morgan's text has been revised and updated to reflect some of the changes our language has undergone in the past two decades. The bibliographic references following each chapter have been completely redone to include a sampling of the many fine books on the New Testament published in the intervening years. The essential content of the book, however, remains the same, as relevant today as it was when it was first published.

It is our hope that *The Layperson's Introduction to the New Testament* will continue to be a valuable resource for many years to come.

The Editors

CONTENTS

INTRODUCTION

This little book is intended as an introduction to the New Testament. Since there are already many such books available, an author must offer valid reasons for the publication of another.

Most standard New Testament introductions fit into one or the other of two classifications: (1) technical works—written primarily for the ordained pastor or seminarian; or (2) reading guides—usually devotional in nature, intended for the layperson as a stimulus to the regular reading of the Bible. Experience has shown that between the readers of these two types of books there is an ever-growing number of men and women (many of them with training in college courses in religion) who find the first type of introduction confusing and the other inadequate. In this age of rapid change and weakening moral and religious foundations, the New Testament, as the fountain of the Christian faith, is the object of much critical examination. Unfortunately, much of this examination not only begins with an unsympathetic spirit, but also with wrong presuppositions and inadequate tools. This book is intended chiefly for those men and women who seek answers to questions about the New Testament that are not easily given in the usual services of worship or study.

The order in which the material is presented differs from that usually found in other books on this subject. The more technical introductions usually present their subjects in what is known as "logical" order, that is, *General Introduction*, including canon, text, life of Christ, and other related general subjects. This is usually followed by *Special Introduction*, which takes up the study of individual books and special problems related to groups of books, such as the Synoptic Gospels. On the other hand, the more devotional introduction usually follows the order of books found in our English Bible in the presentation of its subject matter.

Since this book seeks to show the New Testament as part of the ongoing life of the witnessing church, the material is arranged for study in the probable chronological order of the writing of the books. It is generally agreed that the New Testament books were written some years after the ascension of Christ and the establishment of many scattered missionary congregations. The missionary letters and the Gospels had special meaning for these infant churches which cannot be ignored if one is to understand their purpose. It is self-evident that the church did not come into existence as the result of a study of the New Testament or the decree of a council, but through the work of Spirit-filled Christians. It was these same Christians and the same Spirit who produced the New Testament as a tool for witnessing to the world. When an interpretation fails to take into account this living situation, it is likely to be lame, if not entirely dead.

Questions for discussion have been included with each chapter since it is hoped that this book may be used in adult church school classes, teacher training classes, lay education opportunities, and other appropriate groups. The purpose of such questions is to stimulate discussion, not to project answers. For this reason, some of the questions have been sharpened to the point of being disturbing to provoke serious thought.

The chapter on the text of the New Testament is in some ways the most important in the book and at the same time the one that shows most clearly the limitations of space. Perhaps its very inadequacies may stimulate the reader to further study in special books devoted to this most important subject.

The ultimate aim of author and publisher is to lead the reader to understand the New Testament better and through this deeper understanding of these living words to become better acquainted with the Living Word, whom to know and serve is life eternal.

1

JESUS CHRIST,
THE LIVING WORD

People have approached the task of telling the story of Jesus in many different ways. Some have put the major emphasis on Jesus' skill as a teacher and have presented him as a kind of Christian philosopher who used the questioning method of Socrates as he went about Judea engaging men and women in spiritual dialogue. Others have laid great stress on his understanding of the human personality and have thought of him as a Christian psychologist or the first physician to use the principles of psychosomatic medicine. Still others have seen him as a Christian Gnostic whose real message is to be discovered beneath the surface of his seemingly simple words. Jesus has, at one time or another, been painted as a tragic, romantic, divine, human, gregarious, lonely, simple, or highly complex personality.

All of these approaches have had scholarly advocates and scholarly opponents, for it is not easy to tell in simple terms the story of the One who made so profound an impact on the world. This brief chapter, therefore, will not attempt to relate the story of Jesus nor will it make any claim to having discovered the *one* and *best* way to tell it. It will attempt merely to point out certain aspects of the life and teachings of Christ that assumed major importance in the thinking and preaching of the early church, and thus became the core of the whole of the New Testament.

THROUGH THE EYES OF
THE APOSTLES

The New Testament is the word of God in human language. God might have chosen to reveal Christ in some such miraculous way as is claimed for the Koran and certain other ancient writings, but God chose rather to speak through believers guided by the Holy Spirit in their midst. Since the followers of Jesus believed themselves to be the recipients of the Spirit, it followed that they also believed that they spoke and wrote under the guidance of that same Spirit. It is equally true that they believed themselves to be the real authors of what they wrote, not mere transcribers. The reader of the Gospels should remember also that these accounts are not stenographic reports of events in the life of Jesus, "written up" within a few hours of their occurrence, as is the case in a modern newspaper. While it is possible that some of the followers of Jesus may have made notes when Jesus was still with them, and even written rather full accounts of particular events, this does not seem very likely; nor is there any hint in the New Testament that a serious attempt was made to tell the story of Jesus *in writing* until a generation after his ascension. This means at least two things that are most important for a proper understanding of the New Testament: (1) the Gospel accounts, though written in each case by one person, are probably based on the recollections, personal experiences, and (possibly) written notes of many people (see Luke 1:1-4); (2) the events and the words that are recorded are not given as the *whole* story of Jesus (see John 21:25), but are *selected* accounts to be used in the evangelistic proclamation of the gospel message in the early churches.

At first glance, one might assume that these two conditions limit the reliability and value of the Gospel narratives, but quite the opposite is true. The fact that a generation had passed between the occurrence of the events and the appearance of written accounts does not imply a thirty-year period of silence and inactivity. On the contrary, that period was filled with preaching and teaching, and as a result, the various accounts of Jesus went through a sifting process under the guidance of the Holy Spirit. Thus, those accounts that were of major importance were retained.

THE GOSPEL NARRATIVE IS
STEREOSCOPIC

The picture that we have of Jesus of Nazareth in the New Testament is three-dimensional, as though seen through a stereoscope, for it is always viewed by the writers through the twin "eyepieces" of the *cross* and the *empty tomb.* If the life of Jesus were to be viewed only from the vantage point of the cross, he might be seen as the "man of sorrows," "the suffering servant," the misunderstood teacher, the forsaken leader, the one who "had nowhere to lay his head," the rejected Messiah of Old Testament prophecy, the "godly martyr" who suffered agony in loneliness and died on a Roman instrument of torture amid the bitter abuse and hatred of those whom he had come to save. This is important, but it is not enough.

When this same Jesus is seen from the viewpoint of the empty tomb, the picture is brighter. He then is recognized as the "Strong Son of God" who conquered death, who was the popular leader, the "Lord of hosts," the one who dared to attack entrenched wickedness, the "binder of the strong man" and the one who overcame Satan; the one who declared himself to be "the way, the truth, and the life," who was the transfigured Son of the mountaintop and the compassionate and powerful healer in the valley of human need; the one who even on the cross forgave his torturers, who promised new life to the dying thief, and who in the end committed his soul to his heavenly Father. This was he who was "designated Son of God in power according to the Spirit of holiness by his resurrection from the dead, Jesus Christ our Lord" (Romans 1:4).

There have been some interpreters who have dismissed the account of the resurrection as a myth of later invention. Many of these same interpreters, however, have extolled the virtues of the "kindly prophet" who, though a good man, was mistaken, and who eventually yielded up his life on a cross—a martyr to his faith. There also have been those who have wanted to forget the agony of our Lord's humanity and to celebrate Easter without a Good Friday!

The New Testament is not content with either picture by itself, but always sees the *human Jesus* as the *glorious Christ* of Easter morn. For this reason, it should be clear that we do not have anywhere in the New Testament a picture of what some scholars have called "the historical Jesus." This does not in the least mean that the New Testament is not historical; what it does mean is that the viewpoint of the New Testament is always theological; hence, the facts concerning the life of Jesus are not viewed primarily as events in history, but rather as steps in God's plan of redemption.

THE SON AND THE PROPHET

Although the accounts of the birth and childhood of Jesus are meaningful elements of the gospel story, it does not appear that a recital of them formed a regular part of the early apostolic preaching. For the most part the early sermons were evangelistic, and for that purpose the Passion narratives, rather than the Nativity accounts, were of primary importance.

Son of God and Son of David. Mark's Gospel has no mention of the birth of Jesus, and the account found in the Fourth Gospel is summarized in one verse: "And the Word became flesh and dwelt among us, full of grace and truth; we have beheld his glory, glory as of the only Son from the Father" (John 1:14). Matthew's account begins with a genealogy (Matthew 1:1-17) that validates the Davidic lineage of Jesus. The genealogy given by Luke (Luke 3:23-38) also traces the line of Jesus through David, but continues it back through Adam to God. They both tell of the divine conception and the virgin birth (Matthew 1:18-25; Luke 1:26-38). And this concept of Jesus as both Son of David and Son of God runs throughout the entire New Testament.

"A Prophet Mighty in Deed and Word." It was generally assumed by the Jews that with the conclusion of the work of Malachi the voice of prophecy had ceased. The New Testament, however, proclaims the renewal of the prophetic word, first in John the Baptist (Luke 1:14-17), and supremely in Jesus himself (Luke 24:19). It is especially in this sense that the New Testament speaks

of John as the "forerunner" of Jesus. Jesus did not carry out his earthly ministry as a priest in the temple, or as a rabbi or teacher (although he was called both), but as one in the line of the prophets who came with revelations of new truth, and who based their authority on "Thus saith the Lord." The message of John was: "Repent, for the kingdom of heaven is at hand" (Matthew 3:2). Jesus echoed the same words (Matthew 4:17), but with far deeper meaning, since he who proclaimed the kingdom was the king. John was the *voice;* Jesus was the *Word.*

THE PROCLAMATION OF
THE KINGDOM

Since nearly all of the teachings of Jesus centered upon the idea of the kingdom of God, it may be said that to understand the meaning of the kingdom is to understand the teachings of Jesus.

The Kingdom of God in the Hope of the Jews. It is well known that the fundamental idea of Hebrew religion was that Israel was God's people. Thus, the descendants of Abraham regarded themselves as the people through whom the will of God was to be realized on earth. Through good times and bad, at the height of national prosperity or when prostrate under the conqueror's heel, they never completely abandoned the idea that someday "better times" would come, and that the nation at last would be what God intended it to be.

During most of the Old Testament period, the concept of the kingdom was materialistic and almost exclusively nationalistic. In this view of the kingdom, the individual had little place. Because this nationalistic kingdom was one of time and space, the dead, however righteous their lives had been, could not hope to participate in its messianic age (see 1 Thessalonians 4:13). But with the rise of the great eighth-century prophets—Amos, Micah, and Isaiah—a profound change took place. Preaching as they did, in an age of much material prosperity, they emphasized constantly that God was more concerned with the spiritual nature of people than with the rich gifts that were placed on the altar (see Amos 5:14-15, 21, 27; Micah 6:6-8, and so forth).

During the period of the Exile, when national hopes were at

their lowest ebb, the old nationalistic hopes of an earthly kingdom underwent a great change. Under the leadership of the later prophets, notably Ezekiel and Jeremiah, the idea of religion as personal communion with God was clearly expressed. This idea, where it was accepted, led to revolutionary changes in the concept of the kingdom; for if the center of religion is personal communion with God, then the kingdom must transcend the limits of time and space. Yet, in spite of this, the average Jew at the opening of the first century of the Christian era still saw the hoped-for kingdom as earthly and nationalistic; its blessings were reserved for the descendants of Abraham. For those outside Israel, there was reserved only the wrath of God.

The Kingdom of God in the Teaching of Jesus. The Synoptic Gospels (Matthew, Mark, and Luke) begin their narration of the public ministry of Jesus with his arrival in Galilee, where his opening message was: "The time is fulfilled, and the kingdom of God is at hand; repent, and believe in the gospel" (Mark 1:15). In the parallel passage in Matthew (Matthew 4:17), Jesus says: "The kingdom of heaven is at hand." The two expressions, "kingdom of God" and "kingdom of heaven," are identical in meaning, though Matthew, in deference to Jewish reluctance about using the name of God, prefers generally to employ the term "heaven" (Matthew 5:33-37).

In Luke's Gospel, the temptation of Jesus is followed by the account of his "sermon" in the synagogue of Nazareth (Luke 4:16-30). The lesson that Jesus read, Isaiah, chapters 58 and 61, closed with the words "to proclaim the acceptable year of the Lord." These passages speak clearly of the reign of the Messiah, and referring to them Jesus said: "Today this scripture has been fulfilled in your hearing." His Jewish audience could not mistake his meaning: the reign of the Messiah, toward which the prophets had looked with longing eyes and which John the Baptist had declared to be "at hand," *had actually come.* The age of the Messiah had dawned; the Messiah was in their midst!

Though the words were startling, those who heard them must have been disappointed, for as they looked about, they saw none of their nationalistic dreams of earthly grandeur realized. For them nothing was changed; Jesus knew, however, that *everything* was changed, for the eternal order of God had broken into time and into the affairs of human beings to bring about the culmination of God's redemptive plan.

Many of the popular misconceptions of that day still exist. Even today people speak of "entering the kingdom," as though the kingdom were some club; or they talk of "spreading the kingdom" or "building the kingdom," as though it were restoring the kingdom of David (Acts 1:6). Jesus, in his teaching, never suggested any of these ideas. He taught that the kingdom is the rule of God in the hearts of believers; it is a free gift, something that humankind cannot build, but which becomes a reality when accepted through penitence and faith. This faith that characterizes women and men of the kingdom is not a mere mental acceptance of certain propositions about Jesus, but it is a full commitment of one's life to the lordship of Jesus. While the kingdom is and will always remain the free gift of God, there is laid on humanity the awesome responsibility of accepting it or rejecting it and of ordering one's life by kingdom ideals.

MIRACLES OF CHRIST

Miracles as Signs of the Kingdom. Even the casual reader of the New Testament recognizes that the Gospels picture Jesus as a miracle worker. The logic of this, however, is often missed unless one notices that in John's Gospel miracles are called "signs" (John 2:11, 18; 20:30). If, as Jesus asserted, the kingdom had already come and God's creation had entered into the "last days," it would be natural to expect of Jesus superhuman works as signs of his messianic power. John (in Revelation 11:15) put the basic idea in these words: "The kingdom of the world has become the kingdom of our Lord and of his Christ, and he shall reign for ever and ever." In this passage John is not writing of some far-off time; but, as a pastor concerned for his beloved flock, he is reminding them that the reign of God *has begun.* The miracles of Christ, then, must be seen as normal evidences of the new age and of the presence of its Lord, rather than as occasional and unusual displays of his power. For those who are troubled about the miracles in this "age of science," it may be helpful to point out that the miracle of the incarnation is fundamental, and that the one who accepts this will not boggle at lesser works.

The Twelve Heralds of the Kingdom. Just as there were twelve patriarchs in the old Israel, so there were twelve apostles in the new Israel. This choice of twelve men was the beginning of the kingdom community, or of what became known a little later as the "church" or "called-assembly" of God. The Twelve were not just any men, but undoubtedly were representative of the pious "remnant" in Israel, for at least two of them had been followers of John the Baptist before they came to be with Jesus. Not only were these men given extended explanations of what Jesus was teaching the crowds, but also there were special times (for example, Matthew 16:13-28) when the Lord interrupted his regular program to take them apart for special training. Though they often misunderstood their Master and seemed slow to grasp his true identity, with the descent of the Holy Spirit at Pentecost they began to live and to speak as kingdom men—and the world stopped to listen.

JESUS AS AN ETHICAL TEACHER

There is a certain sense in which we may say that Jesus never taught a system of ethics. Whereas all ethical systems assume that human beings by their own striving can attain to the "good life," it is clear that Jesus regarded sinful humanity as utterly without power to achieve a standard of life that would be pleasing to God. It was for this reason, perhaps more than for any other, that Jesus aroused the hostility of the Pharisees, whose whole religious philosophy was based on the conviction that by keeping the Law they could satisfy God's demands. It was in this spirit that the rich young ruler came to Jesus with the salutation "Good Master." To this, our Lord replied: "No one is good but God alone" (Luke 18:18-19). The implication of the young man's question was that Jesus had achieved goodness and, therefore, could show others how to do so. Jesus understood the implied request, and pointed out to the young man that in calling him "good" he was making him equal with God, since only God is truly good.

The so-called ethical teachings of Jesus are but an extension of Jesus' call to accept the reign of God and seek to follow God in all of life. There is no indication that Jesus ever thought that anyone outside the kingdom could "live by the Sermon on the Mount." Its precepts are not laws to be obeyed or even ideals by which to live, but are illustrations of what *God can do* in the life of one who has accepted the kingdom.

THE PREACHING OF THE EARLY CHURCH

At the very heart of sin is self-centeredness which resents the appeal of God for total self-commitment. Since the people of Jesus' day were sinful, it was, humanly speaking, inevitable that their resentment would end in the use of force to bring Jesus to the cross. Yet the New Testament never pictures Jesus as a martyr who died for a good cause or as a pawn moved by blind fate, but always as one who in spite of sinful humanity fulfilled the plan of divine love. The New Testament does not ask *how* the cross made possible the fulfillment of God's love, but asks persons to *look at the cross*, and with the eyes of faith see that by it God was doing for human beings what they could never do for themselves. There can be no gospel without the cross at the center, even though the redeemed may never fully comprehend its meaning.

As the Gospel writers looked back from the vantage ground of some thirty years of experience and reflection, they could see, though they had not understood it during their association with Jesus, that death could not overcome the Son of God. Hence, Luke writes: "Thus it is written, that the Christ should suffer and on the third day rise again from the dead, and that repentance and forgiveness of sins should be preached in his name. . . ." (See Luke 24:46-47.) Thus, the preaching of the early church had these two foci: the cross and the resurrection. Undoubtedly those early preachers had many other helpful things to say to their listeners, as do their modern successors; but when the gospel is proclaimed in New Testament terms, it tells of a Christ who died and who rose again that we also may die to sin and rise to newness of life.

- What does it mean today to live in "the kingdom of God"?
- What persons or forces in our world are nearest to realizing the ideal of the Sermon on the Mount?

- Why would the Pharisees fear the teachings of Jesus?
- What is the relation between God's gift of the kingdom and the struggle of humankind for freedom?

Additional Resources

Bornkamm, Gunther, *The New Testament: A Guide to Its Writings.* Philadelphia: Fortress Press, 1973.

Drane, John W., *Introducing the New Testament.* New York: Harper & Row, Publishers, Inc., 1987.

Grant, Robert M., *Early Christianity and Society.* New York: Harper & Row, Publishers, Inc., 1977.

Guthrie, Donald, *New Testament Introduction.* Downers Grove, Ill.: Inter-Varsity Press, 1970.

Harrington, Daniel J., *Interpreting the New Testament: A Practical Guide.* Wilmington, Del.: Michael Glazier, Inc., 1979.

Hunter, Archibald M., *The Work and Words of Jesus,* rev. ed. Philadelphia: The Westminster Press, 1973.

Kee, Howard C., *Understanding the New Testament,* 4th ed. Englewood Cliffs, N.J.: Prentice-Hall Inc., 1983.

Ladd, George E., *The Presence of the Future: The Eschatology of Biblical Realism.* Grand Rapids, Mich.: William B. Eerdmans Publishing Co., 1974.

Lohse, Eduard, *The First Christians.* Philadelphia: Fortress Press, 1983.

Marshall, I. Howard, *The Origins of New Testament Christology.* Downers Grove, Ill.: Inter-Varsity Press, 1977.

Neill, Stephen, *Jesus Through Many Eyes: Introduction to the Theology of the New Testament.* Philadelphia: Fortress Press, 1976.

Stott, John R. W., *Basic Introduction to the New Testament.* Grand Rapids, Mich.: William B. Eerdmans Publishing Co., 1964.

2

PREACHING
THE WORD

The Acts of the Apostles begins with a summary of the interval between the resurrection and the ascension of Jesus, a period sometimes called "The Forty Days' Ministry." It is a mysterious season about which little information is given; however, Luke indicates that its importance lay in what the disciples saw and heard (Luke 1:1-11). In the first place, they not only saw Jesus after his resurrection, but their contacts with him extended over a considerable period of time, with the result that any question about the reality of his earlier appearances was banished. In addition to seeing Jesus alive, they heard him speak again about the kingdom of God; his every word became engraved on their memory with meaning greatly enriched by the fact of his resurrection. The climax came when, after commanding them to wait for the power of the Spirit, he departed from them. We have no way of knowing precisely how long they waited in Jerusalem, but we do know that they accepted the responsibility that Jesus had laid upon them, and, like soldiers preparing for battle, they selected Matthias to fill the vacancy left by Judas, so that in numbers as well as in spirit they might be equal to the task given them by their Lord.

IN THE BEGINNING WAS
THE SERMON

As has been well said: "Jesus came not simply to preach the gospel, but that there might be a gospel to preach." The Living Word, then, is both the reason for preaching and the subject of it.

The preaching of the apostles and their followers did not begin with the selection of texts from a book, not even from the Old Testament, but with the proclamation of the mighty acts of God in Christ—acts they themselves had witnessed (1 John 1:1-4). These "mighty acts" were the means of humanity's redemption, and the telling of them was the "Good News," that is, the gospel.

The Period of the Oral Gospel. The Greek word for "gospel" is *evangelion,* from which we derive the meaning "the good news." As originally used in Greek literature, the word meant a reward given to one who brought good news. In later usage it came to mean the good news itself, and it is in this sense that it is used in the New Testament. Our English word "gospel" comes from the Anglo-Saxon *godspel,* which means "good story" or "God story."

During the first Christian generation, about A.D. 30–60, there was little Christian literature in general church use, and almost certainly no written gospel. Nevertheless, before there were written Gospels, the church had a gospel that already had been spread far beyond the boundaries of Palestine and had led to the establishment of many churches. It is most important for a proper understanding of the New Testament to remember that the New Testament came into existence as a result of the gospel and as a means of proclaiming the gospel, but was not itself the source of the gospel.

The Contents of the Oral Gospel. The gospel message that was preached during this period is often called the *kerygma,* from the Greek word meaning "that which is proclaimed." Some idea of this *kerygma* can be formed from a study of the sermons in the Acts and in the letters of Paul. Though not all scholars agree, six major emphases are recognized by all:

1. The future age, prophesied in the Old Testament, has arrived (Acts 2:16; 3:18).
2. This age has dawned through the birth, ministry, death, and resurrection of Jesus, who is the Messiah, born of David's line (Acts 2:22, 24-31).
3. Jesus was raised from the dead and exalted to the place of heavenly power (Acts 2:32-33; 3:13; 5:31).

4. The gift of the Holy Spirit to the church is a sign of this power and of the glorification of Christ (Acts 2:33).
5. Christ will come again in glory to judge humanity (Acts 3:21).
6. In view of what God has done, let all repent and be baptized "unto the remission of sins" (Acts 2:38; 3:19; 4:12; 5:31).

While all of these references are taken from sermons by Peter, it is clear from similar passages in the letters of Paul and in other New Testament writings that this was substantially the gospel message that was proclaimed by all of the first-century preachers. Individual preachers might differ in details, as they added material drawn from their own recollection, but the central theme was essentially the same wherever it was preached. If, by faith, a person accepted these statements as true and took the "yoke of Christ" (Matthew 11:29), he or she was regarded as a follower of "the Way" (Acts 9:2) or, in later terms, a Christian (Acts 11:26).

The Form of the Oral Gospel. While the main elements in the content of the oral gospel seem clear, we know very little of the *form* of those early sermons. Those given in the Acts are, of course, mere outlines, and Luke notes that Peter "testified with many other words and exhorted them . . ." (Acts 2:40). We can guess that among those "many other words" were incidents from the life of Christ, parables, miracles, teachings, and especially interpretations of the Old Testament in the light of the fuller revelation in Christ (1 Corinthians 10:11). While it seems certain that the Passion narrative formed the core of the apostolic preaching, it would be unrealistic to assume that this story was told in isolation; rather, it was thought of as the climax of the wonderful life that had preceded it. The belief that the life of Jesus was no ordinary life but was the life of the incarnate Son of God, gave reason for treasuring his every word. Often what one preacher did not remember concerning Jesus, another did. Some portions of this "word" may have been put in writing at a very early date, even though most people, like Bishop Papias, preferred "the living and abiding voice."

The Selection of Material. The Christians of that day and this believe that the Holy Spirit is at work in the church, and it must be assumed that the Spirit was active in the entire process by which the gospel record was selected and preserved. But God, in wisdom, chose to work through human beings to give to the world a written record of God's saving revelation. We speak of the work of these Spirit-filled believers when we inquire how they came to select certain incidents and to omit others out of a full ministry of several years. Two reasons immediately suggest themselves: (1) controversy with opponents, especially with the Jews, and (2) the practical needs of a rapidly growing community of believers.

Almost from the beginning, Jesus met with opposition from the Jewish community. To understand this opposition, it must be remembered that Jewish teaching of that period assumed that the age of prophecy was past and that the *Torah,* that is, the Law, had taken its place. The scribes delighted in quotations from ancient authorities, but they considered any contemporary who spoke "as having authority" to be presumptuous. Indeed, the Pharisees saw in one who claimed to be a prophet a menace to their neat system of legalism. The Sadducees, the party to which many of the priests belonged, regarded a prophet as a dangerous revolutionary who might undermine the people's loyalty to the temple. Prophets were not popular with the leaders of organized religion (see Luke 4:24).

Since the apostles claimed to be prophets of the "New Israel," they met with the same opposition as had their Master before them. This Jewish opposition made it necessary for Christian preachers to make constant reference to the Old Testament, especially to the later prophets and the messianic Psalms. But the heart of the Christian message, and therefore the chief point of attack, was the Passion narrative, which their Jewish opponents regarded as false and blasphemous. This bitter opposition to that which was at the very center of the gospel may help us understand why so much space is devoted to it in the written Gospels.

A second factor in the molding of the form of the oral gospel was the special need of the Christian community as it attempted to live the life "in Christ." For this reason the New Testament epistles usually contain a fairly equal division of that which might be called "theological" and that which might be called "practical." Because of this constant need for spiritual guidance in matters of everyday living, it is easy to understand why the early church would seek to preserve any words of Jesus that might help in those matters. The large amount of space—three chapters in Matthew's Gospel—given to the Sermon on the Mount may be a reflection of this concern.

NEXT CAME THE SCHOOL

Up to this time we have been thinking of the very first activities of the apostles and their followers. They had a wonderful message to proclaim, and they preached it with fervor and effectiveness. These early evangelists soon realized, however, that converts—especially those from pagan homes—needed more instruction than itinerant preachers could give them. The answer to their need was a teacher and a school. In the beginning was the sermon; next came the school.

The Catechist or Teacher. In Acts 13 Luke tells the story of the sending out of the first missionaries, Saul and Barnabas. In the King James Version, verse 5 reads: "And when they were at Salamis, they preached the word of God in the synagogues of the Jews; and they had also John to their minister." This obscure last phrase is translated in the Revised Standard Version, "to assist them." While this makes better sense than the old version, it still does not convey the full meaning of Luke's words. The difficulty arises from the word used by Luke to describe John Mark's function. It is not a common word in the New Testament, and in ordinary Greek usage meant originally an "under-rower," in contrast to a "seaman." A clue to its New Testament meaning is given in Luke 4:20, which refers to the synagogue "attendant" who cared for the sacred scrolls. This "attendant" (Hebrew *chazzan*), however, had other functions, chief of which was teaching in the synagogue school. If this is what Luke means by the term in Acts 13:5, then John Mark was the *teacher* who instructed those converted under the preaching of the two evangelists, Saul and Barnabas. The importance of the teaching function is emphasized by the differences that later separated Paul and Barnabas. Though the two preachers failed to agree as to the dependability of Mark, it was important for each of them to have with him a teacher. Paul accordingly took Silas with him, and Barnabas took John Mark (Acts 15:36-41).

The Influence of the Teacher on the Form of the Gospel. It is well known that in ancient preliterate societies people often developed remarkable powers of memory. This same enlargement of the power of memory has often been found among the illiterate of all ages. The Jewish society of the first century was neither preliterate nor illiterate, but the common practice of teaching was by rote memory, a practice that helped in the development of that faculty. Furthermore, the educational theory of the day required that the pupil not only memorize the *content* but also the *form,* for the basis of instruction was the sacred Scriptures, where both content and form were accepted as equally inspired. It is undoubtedly true that this attitude toward the Old Testament and the great emphasis placed on verbatim memorization had much to do with the development of the form of the gospel message in the early period. Commenting on this, R. O. P. Taylor gives as his conclusion:

> It is therefore clear that the salient incidents of the gospel history must have been cast into fixed forms as soon as ever there were earnest proselytes and that those episodes would retain those fixed forms because of the national system of teaching.[1]

In the nineteenth century, certain scholars—Godet, Westcott, Salmon, and others—believed that the entire gospel story achieved a fixed form in oral tradition and that the written Gospels were exact copies of this oral gospel. While this theory, as a way of explaining likenesses and differences between the Synoptic Gospels, has been largely abandoned, this does not at all preclude the possibility of the existence of a short Gospel such as Mark in complete and oral form. It is important to emphasize again that the transmission of the gospel by means of oral tradition does not mean that it was subject to the whims and free-editing of the person who transmitted it. Content and form always went together, and the form fixed in oral tradition was no more subject to change than that which was put in writing. This rigidity of form is strikingly illustrated in an article by George Kent in which he recounts the researches of the Grimm brothers in folklore:

The Grimms' best source turned out to be a tailor's wife. Not only did she tell her stories well, but she told them each time in exactly the same words. If she went too fast and was asked to repeat, she would tell them slowly, without change.[2]

The Early Written Gospel. No one knows who first put into writing some word or incident from the life of Jesus, but it may well have been while our Lord was still living on this earth. The age of the oral gospel did not suddenly cease, to be followed immediately and exclusively by written material, but rather the one gradually merged into the other. Written Gospel accounts came into existence while the oral form was still dominant, and oral forms continued for many years after written accounts were commonly used. So long as the apostles and other followers of Jesus were still living and preaching, the church felt little need for written accounts, but by the middle of the first century those first disciples were widely scattered; some had already died (James—to mention but one—in A.D. 44), so that the "living and abiding voice" was soon to be stilled. Then it was that the Christian community first felt the urgency to put into writing the Good News, that for all time people might hear and be saved.

- What is meant by the statement: "There was a gospel before there were Gospels"?
- How were the preaching and teaching ministries of the early church related? How can we improve their relationship today?
- How has the place of preaching changed since New Testament times?
- What reforms are needed today in the teaching ministry of the church?

Additional Resources

Hunter, Archibald M., *Introducing the New Testament,* rev. ed. Philadelphia: The Westminister Press, 1958.
Stonehouse, Ned B., *Origin of the Synoptic Gospels.* Grand Rapids, Mich.: William B. Eerdmans Pub. Co., 1963.

3

MISSIONARY OUTREACH AND THE WRITTEN WORD

Galatians and First and Second Thessalonians

If one were to judge the New Testament from a purely human point of view, one might say that the writing began entirely by accident with no thought of producing a permanent record of God's revelation in Christ. The story of the beginning of the New Testament put in simplest terms is this: A Christian evangelist in the Syrian city of Antioch had just received disturbing news from several of his recent converts. Fearful lest their faith be weakened before he could visit them again, he wrote them a rather long letter of both rebuke and encouragement emphasizing that salvation was by grace through faith and not by human works.

This Christian evangelist was the apostle Paul; the letter was to become known as the Epistle to the Galatians, and the date was A.D. 48 or 49, just twenty years after the close of our Lord's earthly ministry. Though there are many who would argue that Paul's letters to the Thessalonians were the first to be written, the weight of scholarly opinion now seems to favor the letter to the Galatians. In this simple, practical way began the writing of the most precious book in the Christian world, the revelation of the grace of God to sinful humanity as seen in the work and words of the incarnate Son of God.

The Church at Antioch Has a Vision. From the very beginning, Christianity was a missionary faith, but it took some time for the disciples, especially those of Jewish background, to lift their sights from Judea and Samaria to view the whole world as a field for their labors. Luke's second volume, the Acts of the Apostles, describes the broadening of this vision and traces some of the activities of

Peter and Paul as they sought to turn what they envisioned into a reality. The first efforts to carry the Good News beyond Palestine came appropriately from a group of preachers and teachers in the Gentile city of Antioch, where the followers of Jesus were first called Christians. In response to the command of the Spirit, they sent three of their dedicated workers—Barnabas, Saul, and John Mark—to proclaim the gospel on the nearby island of Cyprus. As these three men sailed away from the stone pier at Seleucia, the seaport of Antioch, they initiated a new Christian era—that of missionary outreach to the whole world.

Beginning at Salamis on the eastern shore of the island, they went "through the whole island" to Paphos at its western extremity (Acts 13:5-13). Perhaps the original plan called for the completion of their task with the preaching at Paphos, but instead of returning to Antioch, they set sail for the southern coast of the mainland of Asia Minor. There is some reason to believe that the departure from Cyprus may have been due to Paul's illness, perhaps malaria contracted on that marshy island, and that Paul had determined to seek relief in the high country of the mainland (Galatians 4:13-15).

The Cities of Galatia Hear the Gospel. If Paul had contracted "marsh fever," it is easy to understand why he quickly left the low-lying Pamphylian coast and headed for the mountain cities at an elevation of nearly 4,000 feet above sea level. Their first stop was at Perga, the capital of Pamphylia, about 175 miles northwest of Cyprus. Upon arrival there, John Mark, for reasons unknown, left the two evangelists and returned to Jerusalem (Acts 13:13).

The next stop was at Antioch of Pisidia, where Paul and Barnabas—following their usual custom—preached Jesus as the Messiah in the local synagogue (Acts 13:14-47). At first their message was received with enthusiasm, but there were those who rejected the message as a radical departure from established Jewish thought (Acts 13:48-52). Shaking the dust from their feet—a symbolic act, well understood by the Jews, indicating that henceforth the people of that city would be left to go their own way—Paul and Barnabas turned eastward along the great Roman highway to the city of Iconium.

Here in the synagogue there was a ready reception of the gospel, and converts were won to the faith, "both of Jews and of Greeks" (Acts 14:1); but there was also the usual opposition. In spite of it, the missionaries "remained for a long time" (Acts 14:3) until the growing influence of their opponents forced them out.

Journeying eighteen miles eastward they stopped at the Lycaonian city of Lystra. There is no mention of a synagogue at Lystra, and it may be that they had no intention of preaching there, but the healing of a lame man (Acts 14:8-10) so amazed the pagan villagers that the apostles had to remain. After a horrified rejection of pagan worship, Paul found it necessary to preach the gospel of the one true God. Again there was opposition, not, however, from the townspeople, but from Jewish enemies from Antioch and Iconium. Nor did they escape this time as easily as in the past, for Paul was stoned and left for dead outside the city (Acts 14:19). Sympathetic believers, however, nursed Paul back to health and sent him on his way to Derbe, where Paul and Barnabas preached the gospel and "made many disciples" (Acts 14:21). Soon they were retracing their steps to Perga, then on to the seaport of Attalia, from which they sailed home to Syrian Antioch (Acts 14:24-28).

THE EPISTLE TO THE GALATIANS

The First Missionary Furlough. Although this first missionary journey was quite limited in comparison with the later travels of Paul, these pioneer evangelists had covered about 1,400 miles without any of our modern means of transportation, with very little money, and in the face of bitter opposition. The trip may have taken a year or more, and now that it was over, Paul and Barnabas rested with the disciples in Antioch (Acts 14:28). The date of their return cannot be determined definitely because of a difficulty in reconciling the chronology given by Luke in Acts with that given by Paul in Galatians, but it is believed to have been about A.D. 46 or 47.

The Jerusalem Conference. In Acts 15, Luke is chiefly concerned with a meeting of the apostles and elders at Jerusalem to consider problems that resulted from the integration of Jews and Gentiles in the missionary churches. Paul and Barnabas were chosen as representatives of the church at Antioch to attend this important meeting (Acts 15:2). In Paul's letter to the Galatians, he tells of a meeting in Jerusalem to which he and Barnabas went (Galatians 2:1-10). Are these two accounts of the same meeting, or is Paul speaking of a different one? Opinion is divided on this point, but there seems to be no insuperable argument against viewing them as two. If this is done, we have a chronological starting point, for Paul says in Galatians (Galatians 2:1) that he and Barnabas went up to Jerusalem "after the space of fourteen years" (that is, fourteen years after the previously mentioned trip to Jerusalem [Galatians 1:18-24]). This, Paul says, took place three years after his conversion (Galatians 1:18). From other calculations it is believed that the date of his conversion was A.D. 31. When we add three years and fourteen years, we arrive at A.D. 48 as the date of the apostolic conference of Acts, chapter 15. It is the assumption of this book that the letter to the Galatians was written while Paul rested in Antioch (Acts 14:28) *before* the Jerusalem conference mentioned in Acts 15 and Galatians 2:1-10.

Who Were the Galatians? Before we can understand the problems that Paul discussed in this epistle, we must know something of the people to whom it was sent. The term "Galatians" may refer either to those people who were of the Gallic race and whose ancestors migrated into northern and central Asia Minor in the third century B.C., or to the inhabitants of the towns of the southern part of the Roman province called Galatia, which Paul and Barnabas visited on their first missionary journey. Probably it was these latter people, for the most part not Gauls by race, who were addressed in Paul's letter to the "Galatians." This view is known as the "South Galatian" theory.

What Was the Problem in the Galatian Churches? These young Christians soon came under the influence of the same Jewish groups that had persecuted Paul and Barnabas; and, to complicate matters even more, the churches themselves were composed of Jewish and Gentile converts. Under pressure from one or both of these groups, the Galatian Christians had come to believe that keeping the Jewish law was just as essential to their salvation as faith in Jesus Christ.

For centuries there had existed a wall between Jew and Gentile,

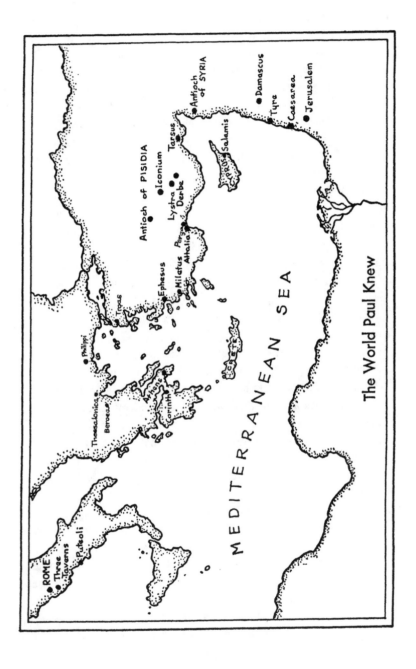

The World Paul Knew

and although Christ had broken down this "middle wall of parti-
tion" (Ephesians 2:14, KJV), it took years before this universal
principle was understood and accepted in the local churches. The
dangerous misunderstanding and lengthy dispute over this matter
is called the Judaizing controversy, and its influence can be seen
in most of the New Testament literature. Paul's letter to the Galatians illustrates the earliest phase of that serious dispute.

Paul's Fight for Freedom from Legalism. From this epistle we
can see that the attack of the Judaizers was directed both at Paul's
apostolic authority and at the validity of his gospel. Four objections to his authority were raised: (1) The Judaizers rejected Paul's
authority on the basis that, since he was not one of the original
twelve, he could not have been appointed by Christ; hence his
gospel rested upon the authority of someone else, probably Peter
(Galatians 1:1, 11-12). (2) They condemned Paul's conciliatory
attitude toward the Gentiles, and insisted that such a policy was
aimed at gaining popularity (Galatians 1:10; 6:17). (3) He was
charged with a policy of vacillation—preaching the keeping of the
law to Jews while discrediting it among the Gentiles (Galatians
5:11). (4) It was said that, since Paul was not an apostle, his gospel
lacked the authority of Peter's and of others of the original twelve
whom the Judaizers claimed to follow (Galatians 1:11-12).

The charges against Paul were serious indeed. If he had com-
promised with the Judaizers, we might never have heard of him
again. But to Paul, compromise in such a matter as faith *versus* law
was unthinkable. Instead, he chose to defend his view of the gospel,
and in so doing wrote his letter which is really a "Declaration of
Independence."

If this letter to the Galatians had been written *after* the Jerusalem conference, as some scholars maintain, it is incredible that it
does not mention the results of that conference. This fact is one
of the strongest arguments for the letter's early date. That momen-
tous meeting came to the conclusion that Gentile converts were
not required to keep such important Jewish requirements as cir-
cumcision, but only to abstain from immorality and to observe
certain minor food laws in deference to their Jewish brethren (Acts
15:28-29). Since both Peter and James, with the Jerusalem elders,

approved of this action, the major argument against the validity of Paul's gospel was demolished.

Paul's argument, however, begins with a defense of his apostolic authority. He rejects emphatically the claim that he was not appointed by Christ (Galatians 1:1, 11-24; 2:11-21). He asserts that prior to his missionary journey his contact with the apostles had been limited to a fifteen-day period (1:18-19), after which he remained in Syria and Cilicia for fourteen years until summoned by Barnabas to assist in the revival at Antioch (1:21; 2:1). Furthermore, Paul points out, "James and Cephas and John . . . gave to me and Barnabas the right hand of fellowship . . ." (2:9b).

From the attack on his authority, Paul turned to defend his concept of the gospel. His argument—and the major theme of the book—consists of a sharp contrast between freedom under grace and bondage under law. It may be summarized as follows: (1) It is grace, working through faith, that saves, so that the true descendants of Abraham are children by faith, not through the flesh (3:7-14). (2) The law became a curse, because it made human weakness clear, but was powerless to help. Christ alone provides a cure for the curse of the law (3:13). (3) God's Son was sent to redeem and to adopt as children those enslaved by the impossible requirements of legalism (4:1-7). (4) The Christian is free, but Christian freedom must be exercised in love (5:1-15). (5) One who is led by the Spirit will show the "fruits of the Spirit" in daily behavior (5:16-24). (6) The true Christian cannot live in isolation, but must assume responsibility for other persons and should begin to exercise this responsibility within the Christian fellowship (6:1-10).

THE SECOND MISSIONARY JOURNEY

At the conclusion of the Jerusalem conference, Paul and Barnabas returned to Antioch, and, after reading the letter from James amid great rejoicing, they gave themselves to teaching and preaching until about the spring of A.D. 49 (Acts 15:30-35). But the missionary spirit was burning in Paul's soul, and after the well-known dispute over whether they should take Mark with them,

Barnabas set out with Mark to Cyprus and Paul went overland, taking Silas with him. After a steep climb through the mountain pass called the Cilician Gates, Paul came once again to the high country of Derbe and Lystra. In one of these two towns (Luke does not make clear which) Paul visited with the family of Timothy. Being much impressed with the lad, Paul persuaded him to accompany them on the journey. Subsequent history proved that Paul's choice of Timothy was one of the wisest and most important he ever made.

The Gospel Comes to Europe. Apparently it was the intention of Paul and Silas to follow the main east-west highway through the province of Asia to Ephesus and the cities of the Lycus valley, but the Holy Spirit in some way not known to us prevented this (Acts 16:7). Changing their direction northward, they headed for the province of Bithynia on the southern shore of the Black Sea. Once again, by divine intervention, their plans were changed. So, turning due west, they came to the seaport of Troas (ancient Troy), not far south of the Hellespont (Acts 16:8).

It was there that Paul saw a vision of a "man of Macedonia" who pleaded with him to "come over to Macedonia and help us" (Acts 16:9). In the next verse the personal pronouns change from the third person ("he" and "they") to the first person plural ("we"). From this it seems clear that Luke joined Paul at Troas, and perhaps it was he who first turned the attention of Paul to the needs of the Greek mainland. The movements of Paul and his associates after leaving Pisidian Antioch show some uncertainty about their missionary objective. They may have been still uncertain when they arrived at Troas and met Luke. Almost certainly Paul, who could quote from the Greek poets (Acts 17:28; Titus 1:12), must have known that he was standing on the ruins of Troy, celebrated in Homer's *Iliad.* This thought, emphasized by the presence of Luke, may have turned Paul's eyes across the sea to that land of glorious history, so proud and yet so poor without Christ! Out of such waking thoughts may have come the vision in the night and the call from God (see Genesis 28:10-22; Acts 10:9-16).

Turning the World Upside Down. In this rapid sketch we cannot stay long with details of how Paul came to Philippi, met Lydia, cast out the evil spirit in the slave girl, and ended up in prison. These facts and his subsequent deliverance are well known. The important thing to be emphasized is that Paul established a church in Philippi which, though poor, was a constant comfort to him, his "joy and crown" (Philippians 4:1).

At the request of the Roman authorities, they were required to leave Philippi, and passing through Amphipolis and Apollonia they came to the capital city, Thessalonica (the modern Salonika). From the brief account in Acts, it would appear that Paul's party stayed in that city for less than a month (Acts 17:2), but in First Thessalonians Paul seems to imply a stopover of considerable duration (1 Thessalonians 2:1-12). Nevertheless, the work at Thessalonica was rudely interrupted (Acts 17:5-9), and Paul along with Silas was hurried out of town to Beroea. Here the same pattern of Jewish opposition developed. Thereupon the brethren, fearing for Paul's life, dispatched him by land and sea out of Macedonia and southward toward Athens, while Silas and Timothy remained in Macedonia to care for the young churches. Though the brief account given by Luke does not impress one with the success of the Macedonian "campaign," it was said of these men that they had "turned the world upside down" (Acts 17:6).

PAUL AT ATHENS

One gets the impression that Paul's visit to Athens was not a part of his missionary plan. He appears to be "marking time" in Athens (Acts 17:16) until favorable word should come from his helpers in Macedonia indicating that it was safe to return. Though the "golden age" of Athens, even in Paul's day, had long since passed, there was, nonetheless, much of beauty and wisdom in that noble city to attract anyone. Perhaps Paul was sightseeing, tourist-like, when his eye caught sight of an altar dedicated "to an unknown god." He was greatly disturbed by the idolatry all about him, and using this inscription from a pagan altar as his text and the Areopagus as his pulpit, he proclaimed the one true God as revealed in Jesus Christ (Acts 17:22-31) to an audience that was always waiting to listen to any new and often strange doctrine.

When Paul preached Jesus and the resurrection, his hearers may have thought that he was speaking of some god named Jesus and of a female consort, a goddess named *Anastasis* (Greek for "resurrection"). When they understood him better, most of them mocked (Acts 17:32), but certain of them, known by name to Luke, believed. Nothing further is told of these converts, nor does the New Testament mention a Christian church at Athens.

FIRST AND SECOND THESSALONIANS

From Athens Paul continued his journey southward to Corinth, the cosmopolitan and dissolute capital of the province of Achaia. Here he found congenial companions and fellow tentmakers in Aquila and Priscilla, with whom he lived and worked for about eighteen months. On the basis of important archaeological discoveries, it is possible to date Paul's arrival at Corinth with unusual accuracy. Gallio was proconsul of Achaia from the summer of A.D. 51 (some scholars say 50) to the summer of A.D. 52 (some say 51); and since Paul was tried before this same Gallio (Acts 18:12-17), he must have arrived at Corinth about a year earlier, that is, in the late summer or fall of A.D. 50, or a year before. With this information we can date other trips by Paul.

While Paul was working at Corinth, Silas and Timothy arrived from Macedonia with a mixture of good news and bad news (Acts 18:5; 1 Thessalonians 3:6-7). Paul was overjoyed to hear that the little group of believers with whom he had stayed such a short time had remained steadfast, but he was troubled that they had greatly misunderstood his teaching about the coming kingdom. They had been taught that by faith they would share in the blessings of the coming kingdom, but apparently they had assumed that these blessings would be enjoyed only by those alive at Christ's coming. Because some of their number had died since accepting Paul's teaching, the living were deeply concerned over their future state. To this Paul replied with assurances that Christians, whether living or dead, would participate on equal terms in the coming kingdom at the advent of Christ.

The effects of this first letter were hardly what Paul had anticipated. Some of the Thessalonians, understanding from Paul's letter that the kingdom was to come soon, had quit their usual occupations and were awaiting the Lord's return in idleness, even behaving in a disorderly manner (2 Thessalonians 3:6-13). Whereupon Paul wrote again, probably not more than three months after his first letter, to clarify their misunderstanding and to warn them against evil conduct. After expressing his thanks for their faith (2 Thessalonians 1:1-12), he explained that some time must elapse before the coming of the Lord (2:1-12). He then exhorted them to stand fast (2:13-17) and, after a brief prayer (3:1-5), urged them to be patient and continue their work (3:6-15). In his conclusion he called attention to his own handwriting as evidence of the authenticity of the letter (3:16-18). The date of these two letters cannot be later than the fall and winter of A.D. 50, and they may have been written a year earlier.

- What do you think of Paul's missionary strategy in establishing churches in large cities and beginning his work in Jewish synagogues?
- How do you interpret the relationship between law and grace?
- What should you do when you disagree with doctrines held by other Christians?
- How do these letters speak to us and our world?

Additional Resources

Barrett, C. K., *Freedom and Obligation: A Study of the Epistle to the Galatians.* Philadelphia: The Westminster Press, 1985.

Best, Ernest, *The First and Second Epistles to the Thessalonians,* New Testament Commentaries Series. New York: Harper & Row, Publishers, Inc., 1972.

Bornkamm, Gunther, *Paul.* New York: Harper & Row, Publishers, Inc., 1971.

Bruce, Frederick F., *The Epistle to the Galatians.* Grand Rapids, Mich.: William B. Eerdmans Publishing Co., 1982.

Bruce, Frederick F., *Paul and His Converts: 1 and 2 Thessalonians, 1 and 2 Corinthians.* Nashville: Abingdon Press, 1962.

Bruce, Frederick F., *Paul and Jesus.* Grand Rapids, Mich.: Baker Book House, 1974.

Bruce, Frederick F., *The Pauline Circle.* Grand Rapids, Mich.: William B. Eerdmans Publishing Co., 1985.

Goodspeed, Edgar J., *The Story of the New Testament,* 2nd ed. Chicago: University of Chicago Press, 1929.

Keck, L. E., *Paul and His Letters.* Philadelphia: Fortress Press, 1979.

Lewis, E. R., *Acts of the Apostles and Letters of St. Paul.* London: James Clarke & Co., 1960.

Longenecker, R. N., *New Testament Social Ethics for Today.* Grand Rapids, Mich.: William B. Eerdmans Publishing Co., 1984.

4

PROBLEMS AND
PROFOUND DOCTRINES

First and Second Corinthians and Romans

It appears from Acts that Paul left Corinth shortly after the writing of his second letter to the Thessalonians. Therefore, the total time he spent in Corinth was something over eighteen months (Acts 18:11, 18), at the conclusion of which he sailed home. After brief stops along the way (Acts 18:19), he came to Caesarea and thence to Antioch (Acts 18:22), where he reported to the church and spent some time in a much-needed and well-deserved rest.

Paul was not one to give much time to rest, however, and soon he set out overland to visit the churches in the provinces of Galatia and Phrygia (Acts 18:23; compare 16:6). The highway on which he traveled led eventually to Ephesus, where he lived and preached for more than two years (Acts 19:8-10). Ephesus was not only the major seaport of the province of Asia, but it was also located on or at the terminus of roads leading north, east, and south. Certainly Paul and his companions spent many weary days in travel along these roads as they carried the gospel to the cities and scattered villages in that wide area. Out of this ministry came such churches as those at Laodicea, Smyrna, Sardis, Philadelphia, Thyatira, Pergamos (Revelation 2–3), Colossae, Hierapolis, and others. During this same period Paul may have made even more extensive evangelistic trips which, though not mentioned by Luke in the Acts, are suggested by Paul's own letters (see 2 Corinthians 11:23-28). One such journey was certainly made to Corinth (2 Corinthians 2:1; 12:14), and some scholars believe that the evangelization of Crete may have had its beginning at this time (Titus 1:5).

CORINTH, THE PROBLEM CHURCH

It is impossible to understand adequately the difficulties and dangers that beset the Christian community at Corinth, or the importance Paul attached to that church, unless one has some understanding of the nature and strategic location of the city. A glance at a map of the Greek peninsula will show that the lower third of the land mass is virtually an island, separated from the upper two-thirds by the great arm of the Corinthian Gulf on the west and the Saronic Gulf on the east. In ancient times it was customary for small ships bound for the West to sail up the Saronic Gulf and be hauled overland to the Corinthian Gulf. Corinth, situated a mile and a half south of the isthmus and strongly fortified, commanded all commerce whether by land or by sea. Its population was cosmopolitan, devoted to the licentious worship of Aphrodite, and it was of immoral repute, even by the rather lax standards of ancient paganism. In the language of the ancient world, if one wanted to refer politely to another's immoral actions, one might say that the other behaved "like a Corinthian." Since Paul wrote the letter to the Romans from Corinth, his thorough indictment of sinful humanity (Romans 1:18-32) may have been suggested by the Corinthian scene.

There in that city of wealth, power, influence, and innumerable vices, was a small, struggling, confused, and often sinful group of Christians who were very dear to Paul. They were a test and a challenge. If the grace of God could win in Corinth, it could win anywhere!

In describing Paul's relations with Corinth, Luke mentions two visits and two letters, but the apostle's contacts appear to have been more numerous and more varied than Luke's account would imply. A study of the Acts and the Corinthian epistles suggests the following outline:

1. The first visit and founding of the church   A.D. 50–51
   (Acts 18:1 ff.)
2. The "previous letter" (1 Corinthians 5:9), now lost   53
3. A letter from Corinth (1 Corinthians 7:1 ff.)   55

In addition to the information gained through these visits and letters, Paul had important contacts through his relations with Stephanas, Fortunatus, Achaicus (1 Corinthians 1:16; 16:15-17), and the family of Chloe (1 Corinthians 1:11).

Shortly after the apostle's first visit to Corinth, a crisis developed that was as dangerous as the one he had faced in Galatia. As in Galatia this involved a rejection by some Corinthian Christians of Paul's apostolic authority; but unlike the difficulty in Galatia, the Corinthian church was troubled with gross immorality together with Gentile misunderstandings and various perversions of Christian teaching.

FIRST CORINTHIANS

The letter itself is easily divided into two main sections. After brief greetings (1 Corinthians 1:1-9), Part 1 deals with problems arising out of unchristian conduct (1:10–6:20). Part 2 consists of Paul's answers to their questions (7:1–16:4). The conclusion is found in chapter 16, verses 5 to 24.

Part 1. Unchristian Conduct (1:10–6:20)

1. Factionalism (1:10–4:21). For reasons not clearly known, the church was split into four or more parties. There were the partisans of Paul, of Apollos, of Peter, and a group that claimed to be the "Christ party." Paul's rebuking answer is that Christian leaders are but workers engaged in the common task of building the church on the one foundation which is Christ Jesus (3:5-17).

2. Immorality (5:1-13; 6:12-20). Not only was there immorality in the church (5:1), but it was a form of immorality (incest) that was condemned by pagan as well as Jewish law. Furthermore, the church seemed complacent about the whole matter (5:2). Accordingly, Paul insists with some heat that the church "clean house" and discipline the offenders, as they would do if he were present in person (5:3-7).

3. Litigation in Pagan Courts (6:1-11). Though Greeks were well known for their love of argument and for their frequent participation in lawsuits, Paul was horrified at the thought of a Christian suing another Christian before a non-Christian judge (6:1). He argues that Christian differences should be settled within the church, and if it is believed that a Christian has not received justice, one should be willing to suffer injustice rather than go to a Roman court (6:2-7).

Part 2. Their Questions and Paul's Answers (7:1–16:4)

1. Marriage vs. Celibacy (7:1-40). Revulsion against the low view of marriage that prevailed in their pagan world may have led many Christian converts to consider celibacy as the preferred state. Paul answers the inquiry by saying that "the form of this world is passing away" (7:31b); hence it would be better for them not to make radical changes in social custom.

2. Food Sacrificed to Idols (8:1–11:1). In Corinth, as in most cities of that age, much of the meat that was sold for public use had routinely been offered to a god. Some of the Corinthian Christians doubted the propriety of eating such meat, lest their act be construed as participation in idol worship. Paul's answer is that idols are nothing and that Christians are free from food taboos, but that Christians, in using freedom, must have regard for both their weaker friends and their public witness (8:4, 13, 23).

3. Irregularities in Public Worship (11:2-34). Apparently the Corinthians asked two other questions. First: "Does the new freedom in Christ emancipate women from the custom of wearing a head-covering when appearing in public?" Paul's reply is thoroughly Semitic in its insistence on the subordination of women, but his major concern is that no Christian, by the sudden breaking of local custom, should undermine the Christian witness. The second question apparently was this: "How should one properly observe the Lord's Supper?" It is Paul's view that the need for food should be satisfied at home or in a feast separate from the Communion. Only those who "discern the body" may participate.

4. Spiritual (Charismatic) Gifts (12:1–14:40). The content of these important chapters may be summarized as follows: (1) The gifts of the Spirit are diverse yet unified, like the parts of the body (12:1-30). (2) Seek after the highest gifts: faith, hope, and especially love (12:31–13:13). (3) Speaking for church edification is better than ecstatic experience (speaking in tongues), which benefits only the participant (14:1-25). (4) There should be orderliness in the exercise of all spiritual gifts (14:26-40).

5. The Resurrection and the Resurrection Body (15:1-58). Here Paul deals with the *certainty* of the resurrection (15:1-34) and the *nature* of the new body (15:35-58). While the fact of the resurrection is a fundamental principle of the entire gospel message, its nature and meaning are most fully discussed here.

6. The Collection for the Poor and the Conclusion (16:1-24). Paul urges that they have the collection ready when he arrives. He then outlines some of his plans for future missionary work.

SECOND CORINTHIANS

If we are correct in our interpretation of scattered references in these two Corinthian letters, Paul made another visit to Corinth, after writing First Corinthians (2 Corinthians 2:1; 12:14; 13:1). That visit apparently was highly unsatisfactory, and Timothy's subsequent report increased Paul's concern. The result was that he dispatched Titus to Corinth with a very stern letter (2 Corinthians 2:1-11; 7:8). Sometime later, Paul left Ephesus and awaited the return of Titus in Macedonia. When at last Titus returned and reported a favorable reception of Paul's letter, Paul replied—with a great sense of relief—in a fourth letter, which is our Second Corinthians.

An important question for all who seriously study God's Word is: "What happened to the two 'lost letters' of Paul to Corinth?" Most people are content to admit that they are lost and let the matter drop, but others have maintained that these two letters may be found, wholly or in part, in our Second Corinthians. Behind this theory is the assumption that, when a collection was made of

Paul's letters, First Corinthians was found to fill a papyrus roll of usual length, so the scribe labeled this "Paul, to the Corinthians—1." Since Second Corinthians did not fill the second roll, two other letters (or parts of letters) of Paul to Corinth were included, and the scribe entitled it: "Paul, to the Corinthians—2."

According to this theory, a portion of the "previous letter" is preserved in 2 Corinthians 6:14–7:1, where some have sensed a break in the flow of thought. The theory further suggests that the "severe letter" consists of chapters 10 to 13, as indicated by an abrupt change of tone from relief and joy to severity and rebuke. The arguments for and against this theory do not properly belong in this brief introductory text, but since there is considerable difference of opinion among scholars with respect to this theory, it seems best to accept Second Corinthians as a unit. Perhaps the simplest explanation of the difference in tone is that Paul did not write the whole of Second Corinthians at one sitting or under similar circumstances.

Outline of Second Corinthians

Part 1. (Chapters 1–9)
  a. Salutation (1:1-2)
  b. Trouble and deliverance (1:3-11)
  c. Charges against Paul and refutation (1:12–2:4)
  d. Advice on matters of church discipline (2:5-11)
  e. The ministry of reconciliation (2:12–7:16)

Part 2. (Chapters 8–9)
  a. The collection for Jerusalem and the basic principles of Christian stewardship (Chapters 8–9)

Part 3. (Chapters 10–13)
  a. Paul defends his apostolic authority (10:1-18)
  b. A strong reply to Corinthian critics (11:1–13:4)
  c. Prayer, greetings, and benediction (13:5-14)

Book title:

Your comments:

Where did you hear about this book:

Reasons why you bought this book: (check all that apply) ☐ Subject ☐ Author ☐ Attractive Cover

☐ Recomendation of a friend ☐ Recomendation of a Reviewer ☐ Gift ☐ Other

If purchased: Bookseller _____ City _____ State _____

Please send me a Judson Press catalog. I am particularly interested in: (check all that apply)

1. ☐ African American	5. ☐ Christian Education	9. ☐ Devotional/Prayer
2. ☐ Baptist History/Beliefs	6. ☐ Christian Living	10. ☐ Preaching/Sermon Helps
3. ☐ Bible Study	7. ☐ Church Leadership	11. ☐ Self-Help
4. ☐ Children's Books	8. ☐ Church Supplies	12. ☐ Women's Issues

Yes, add my name to your mailing list!

Name (print) _____

Street _____

City _____ State _____ Phone _____

Please send a Judson Press catalog to my friend:

Name (print) _____

Street _____

City _____ State _____ Zip _____ Phone _____

Name (print) _____

Street _____

City _____ State _____ Zip _____

Judson Press • P.O. Box 851 • Valley Forge, PA 19482-0851 • 1-800-458-3766 • FAX (610) 768-2107

Visit our website at www.judsonpress.com

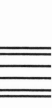

BUSINESS REPLY MAIL

FIRST-CLASS MAIL   PERMIT NO. 6   VALLEY FORGE PA

POSTAGE WILL BE PAID BY ADDRESSEE

JUDSON PRESS

PO BOX 851
VALLEY FORGE PA 19482-9897

FROM EPHESUS TO CORINTH

From 2 Corinthians 1:16 it appears that Paul had originally planned to travel from Ephesus to Corinth by ship, but the increased tenseness of the situation in Corinth changed his plans. As mentioned previously, Paul went overland and, after meeting Titus, spent some time in Macedonia visiting his missionary churches before continuing his journey to Corinth.

One of the reasons for Paul's tour of the churches of Macedonia was to encourage them to give generously to the fund he was collecting for the poor Christians in Jerusalem. Undoubtedly the primary reason for collecting this money was the desperate need of the poor (see Galatians 2:10), but in addition to this, Paul may have hoped that an exhibition of generosity by Gentile Christians would help to heal the differences between Jew and Gentile within the church.

Not only was the taking of this collection one of the important reasons for this mission to the Macedonian churches, but it was also the major reason for Paul's last visit to Jerusalem. When the collection had been completed, the apostle paid his last visit to Corinth, where he hoped to spend the winter. (The statements of Paul [1 Corinthians 16:6] and Luke [Acts 20:3] agree on this.) There, perhaps in the home of Gaius and among many friends, Paul rested, preached, and wrote what many consider to be his greatest work—the letter to the church at Rome.

THE EPISTLE TO THE ROMANS

As we enter upon a study of this most profound letter, two questions immediately suggest themselves: (1) Why did Paul *write* to Rome instead of visiting that city? (2) Why did he write a letter of this character to a congregation composed largely of people unknown to him?

The answer to the first question is relatively simple. Paul's missionary strategy called for the establishment of Christian churches in all of the major cities of the Roman Empire. Furthermore, though his understanding of the gospel was well known in the eastern churches, most of which he had founded, he had not yet had opportunity to present his views to this church which was located at the very crossroads of the Empire. Though he had hoped for many years to visit Rome and was still hopeful of doing so (Romans 1:10-13), he must for the present delay his visit until after he had taken the collection to Jerusalem (Romans 15:25-26). Since a visit was now impossible, a letter was the next best thing.

While the answer to the first question is rather obvious, it is not so easy to understand why Paul wrote this *kind* of letter to the church in Rome. The letters of Paul to the churches of Galatia, Thessalonica, Corinth, Colossae, and Ephesus all reflect certain peculiar needs and problems of those congregations. The Pastoral Epistles and even the tiny letter to Philemon are all specific and quite personal. But, except for its final chapter, the Epistle to the Romans is quite impersonal and devoid of any discussion of problems or specific needs of that church.

Some have suggested that through Priscilla, Aquila, and others from Rome, Paul had learned of Judaizers who were at work in the church and that he wrote in an attempt to head off a serious controversy, such as had almost destroyed the churches of Galatia. While it is true that both the Roman letter and the Galatian letter show the same strong emphasis on the sole sufficiency of grace and the freedom of the believer from law, in Romans this emphasis appears to be an integral part of a larger discussion and is never openly aimed at any party.

Others have argued that this work of Paul is not really a letter—even in the formal sense of that term—but rather a theological treatise in which Paul presents the basic principles on which he based his proclamation of the gospel. Admittedly this profound document exhibits less concern with matters of local or temporary concern, and it also contains the fullest statement of Paul's thought, but these factors are not weighty enough to change the traditional understanding of its epistolary character. Paul's development of the measured, logical argument is often interrupted with expressions of his own deeply personal religious experience, in which he refers to his early inward struggles (for example, in chapters 7 and 9) and passionately affirms his willingness to die for the salvation of his Jewish compatriots.

Still other scholars have suggested that Paul's major purpose may have been to create interest in his proposed mission to Spain (Romans 15:24) in hope that the church at Rome might undertake the support of that mission. Such a purpose, though worthy in itself, does not seem sufficient reason for the urgent character or the profound contents of this letter.

The most satisfactory explanation of why Paul wrote this kind of letter seems to be his desire to challenge this large and strategic church with a comprehensive statement of the universal character of Christianity in contrast with the narrow nationalism of Judaism, especially as found in the views of the Judaizing Christians.

THE MESSAGE OF ROMANS

Archibald Hunter believes that the theme of Romans can be expressed in six words, which he credits to Anderson Scott, namely: "Salvation, its root and its fruit."[3] On the basis of this concise statement, we may outline the epistle as follows:

1. The Root of Salvation (chapters 1–8). After a brief prologue (1:1-15), Paul states his basic principle in verses 16 and 17: "For I am not ashamed of the gospel: it is the power of God for salvation to every one who has faith, to the Jew first and also to the Greek. For in it the righteousness of God is revealed through faith for faith; as it is written 'He who through faith is righteous shall live.' " The quotation is from Habakkuk 2:4, but a comparison of that passage with Paul's statement will reveal the heart of Paul's gospel. The Old Testament passage recognizes a righteousness *apart* from faith, but Paul's use of the passage reflects the Christian understanding that righteousness *comes only* by faith. This was the revolutionary thought that came also to Luther and that became the spark of the Reformation: salvation is by grace through faith, and not by works.

2. The Place of the Jews in God's Plan (chapters 9–11). Here Paul is concerned with the mystery of why God's ancient people rejected their Messiah. His personal longing is that all of them might be saved (10:1), but he is convinced that only the *spiritual* descendents of Abraham can really be called "Jews" (9:6-8). He insists, however, that God has not completely rejected the Jewish people, and that in some way as yet unknown, "all Israel will be saved" (11:26).

3. The Fruit of Salvation (12:1–15:13). The Christian gospel has never been as completely "otherworldly" as some critics have maintained. For Paul, and for all other Christians, the truth is proclaimed not only in order that people might be saved for the world to come but also that they might be "new creatures" in this world. The key verse in these chapters is: "Do not be conformed to this world but be transformed by the renewal of your mind, that you may prove what is the will of God, what is good and acceptable and perfect" (12:2). This entire section constitutes one great trumpet call to noble Christian living as the natural outgrowth of the marvelous grace of God (compare John 15).

• What effect or impact did these early churches have upon their communities and the world?

• How does an understanding of such things as authorship, date, purpose, and readers help us to a deeper comprehension of the gospel message?

• How does Paul use theology to help solve practical problems in the churches? Examine, in particular, First Corinthians. How can we apply this theology to problems in our churches?

Additional Resources

Barclay, William, *The Mind of St. Paul.* New York: Harper & Row Publishers, Inc., 1959.

Barrett, C. K., *The First Epistle to the Corinthians,* New Testament Commentaries Series, vol. 9. New York: Harper & Row, Publishers, Inc., 1968.

Barrett, C. K., *The Second Epistle to the Corinthians.* New York: Harper & Row, Publishers, Inc., 1973.

Barth, Karl, *Epistle to the Romans.* London: Oxford University Press, 1933.

Bruce, Frederick F., *1 and 2 Corinthians,* Grand Rapids, Mich.: William B. Eerdmans Publishing Co., 1971.

Cranfield, C. E. B., *Romans: A Shorter Commentary.* Grand Rapids, Mich.: William B. Eerdmans Publishing Co., 1985.

Dummelow, John R., *Commentary on the Holy Bible.* New York: The Macmillan Co., 1925.

Guthrie, Donald, *The Pauline Epistles,* vol. 1 in *New Testament Introduction.* Chicago: Inter-Varsity Press, 1961.

Hunter, Archibald M., *Introducing the New Testament.* rev. ed. Philadelphia: The Westminster Press, 1958.

Murphy-O'Connor, Jerome, *St. Paul's Corinth.* Wilmington, Del.: Michael Glazier, Inc., 1983.

5

LETTERS FROM
PRISON

Ephesians, Colossians, Philemon, Philippians

Paul's determination to journey to Jerusalem, in spite of repeated warnings of danger (Acts 21:4, 10-13), seems foolhardy unless one understands the depth of Paul's concern for the church. He had taken up a generous collection among the Gentile Christians for the poor at Jerusalem, a collection that he hoped to be able to distribute on the occasion of the Feast of Pentecost (Acts 20:16), perhaps as a reminder of the unity of the church in the Spirit. The warnings of danger only served to remind Paul of the depth of the cleavage in the Christian community between Jew and Gentile. So serious was this breach that the more legalistic Christians might easily have separated at that time and formed a Jewish church in opposition to the more Gentile church that Paul had founded in the provinces. Paul recognized that he had been responsible in large measure for bringing this issue to a head, and consequently he felt that only by his presence in Jerusalem could the split be avoided.

The Suggestion of James and the Jerusalem Elders. Immediately upon his arrival in Jerusalem (Acts 21:18), Paul and his party met with the official leaders of the Jerusalem church. After hearing Paul's report of his recent experiences, James explained that in the Christian community of Palestine there were widespread suspicions about Paul's orthodoxy. Out of the discussion, a plan was developed whereby Paul would associate himself with four Jewish Christians who were about to take a seven-day vow. It was hoped that by paying the expenses of these men and appearing in the temple with them, the suspicions of Paul's attitude toward Jewish customs might be allayed. Apparently, however, opposition to Paul was too deep-seated to be overcome by such an action, and Paul's enemies, on the pretext that Paul had taken a Gentile into the temple, rose up against him, and in the riot that followed, the Roman tribune found it necessary to take Paul into protective custody.

The Caesarean Imprisonment (Acts 21:31–26:32). After a brief stay in the military headquarters at Jerusalem (22:24–23:35), Paul was delivered into the hands of the Roman procurator Felix, in whose prison in Caesarea he languished for two years (24:26). Felix was succeeded by Porcius Festus about A.D. 58. Festus soon learned of the bitter enmity of the Jews toward Paul, and like Felix, probably would have kept Paul in his prison indefinitely if Paul had not exercised his rights as a Roman citizen and appealed his case to the imperial high court at Rome. In spite of the optimistic words of King Agrippa (26:32), in all probability both he and Festus were happy to be rid of so thorny a problem, and they sent Paul off to Rome in the custody of the centurion Julius (27:1).

The Voyage to Rome (Acts 27:1–28:16). Luke appears to have been a companion of Paul during his Caesarean imprisonment, and he may at this time have gathered much of the material for his Gospel, about which more will be said later. The subsequent voyage to Rome, with its great tempest and eventual shipwreck, is told in masterly fashion by Luke as only an eyewitness could relate it (27:21–28:10). Eventually the castaways were rescued and brought to Rome (28:11-16), where Paul was placed under "house arrest" for the two years of his first Roman imprisonment.

WHERE DID PAUL WRITE HIS PRISON LETTERS?

It is the assumption of this author that all four of the Prison Epistles (that is, Ephesians, Colossians, Philemon, Philippians) were written from Rome during the two-year imprisonment mentioned in Acts 28:30-31. No New Testament introduction would be complete, however, which did not recognize that some scholars have suggested Ephesus, Caesarea, or even Philippi as the place of writing.

The theory that they were written during the Philippian imprisonment may be safely dismissed since, according to the Acts, it
lasted hardly more than twenty-four hours. Arguments in favor of
Caesarea as the place of writing have been largely superseded by
those in favor of Ephesus, even though no Ephesian imprisonment
is expressly mentioned in the New Testament. An imprisonment
at Ephesus has been inferred because:

1. In 2 Corinthians 11:23, Paul speaks of himself as having
endured "far more imprisonments" than other Christian missionaries. While one must admit that Paul's expression—"far more
imprisonments"—does argue for more than the three (Philippi,
Caesarea, and Rome) mentioned by Luke, it seems impossible to
fit any one of these "other imprisonments" into Paul's Ephesian
ministry subsequent to the riot (Acts 19:28-41), and there would
be no reason for any incarceration prior to this event.

2. In 1 Corinthians 15:32, Paul speaks of having "fought with
beasts" at Ephesus. Most commentators, however, assume that the
reference is to contests with "beast-like" persons.

3. Paul mentions enduring some great affliction in Asia (2
Corinthians 1:8), and also an occasion when Prisca and Aquila
risked their lives for his sake (Romans 16:3-4). Here again there
is no specific mention of an imprisonment at Ephesus.

4. Clement of Rome (c. A.D. 95) mentions seven imprisonments
of Paul,[4] but he does not list them by name. His statement may
simply be based on Paul's own statement in 2 Corinthians 11:23,
"seven" being the mystical number of completeness.

5. Marcion (c. A.D. 140) states that the letter to the Colossians
was written from Ephesus. Since he also says that the letters to
Philippi and to Philemon were written from Rome, and since the
close relationship of Colossians and Philemon has been definitely
established, it is hard to accept seriously the historical value of the
Marcionite prologue.

Since the evidence includes no certain allusion to an Ephesian
imprisonment, it seems best to accept the traditional view that
these four letters were written during Paul's imprisonment at
Rome.

THE LETTER TO THE EPHESIANS

Theme: Unity in Christ

The exact chronological order in which the four Prison Epistles were written is not known. The only thing certain is that the letter to the Colossians and the letter to Philemon were written and sent at the same time. There are hints in the letter to the Philippians that Paul was expecting an early release from prison, and for this reason we put that letter last, and Ephesians, thought by some to be an introductory letter, we put first.

Destination. During the last century the destination of this letter had been a matter of question for reasons such as the following:

1. Some of the earliest and best manuscripts omit the words "at Ephesus" which appear in Ephesians 1:1 in the King James Version.

2. The letter seems formal and strangely impersonal for one addressed to a congregation with which Paul had lived and worked for more than two years.

3. In Colossians 4:16 mention is made of an epistle from Paul to the church at Laodicea. Some have thought that the letter bearing the title "To the Ephesians" may be the lost letter to the Laodiceans. Marcion called our Ephesians the "Epistle of Paul to the Laodiceans," but he gave no reasons for his choice of that title.

As early as the fifteenth century the scholar Beza suggested that the problem might be solved by assuming that our Ephesians was written as a circular letter, and that Paul entrusted several copies of the letter to Tychicus with instructions to fill in the name of the church to which he delivered each copy. This theory further assumes that the title "To the Ephesians" has been retained in the canon because this was the most influential church in the group.

All of this, however, is conjecture, and until stronger evidence is available, it seems best to assume that Paul wrote this letter to the church at Ephesus, possibly with the hope that its contents would be shared with other churches in the area. Such a theory would account adequately for the somewhat formal tone and lack of personal greetings.

Authorship. Did Paul write this letter? With the exception of Marcion, the early church is unanimous in its acceptance of the Pauline authorship. The question arose in the early days of the scientific study of the literature of the New Testament when the traditional authorship of each book was carefully examined. As a result of the study of Ephesians, the following questions were raised:

1. Is this Paul's usual vocabulary? The letter to the Ephesians contains ninety words not found in Paul's other letters.

2. Is this Paul's style? This epistle contains several long and complex sentences, thought by some scholars to be contrary to Paul's usual style (see Ephesians 1:3-14, which is all one sentence in the Greek).

3. Is there not a change in the meaning of key words? Certain words that are common to Paul's letters, such as "mystery," "body," "fullness," seem to some scholars to have acquired a new un-Pauline meaning.

4. Is this letter in harmony with Paul's doctrine? The doctrine of the universal church is said to contradict Paul's normal reference to "churches."

5. Why would Paul write another letter so similar to Colossians? Ephesians contains more than one-third of the words and phrases found in Colossians. Since Colossians is assumed to be genuinely Pauline, it is alleged that such a versatile writer as Paul would hardly have copied himself to this extent.

These questions are examined in detail in commentaries on Ephesians. Space forbids more than a brief summary defense, which follows the form of that given by Archibald M. Hunter:[5] (1) Ephesians 6:21 seems to have no point unless we assume Pauline authorship. (2) There was complete unanimity in the early church concerning its Pauline authorship, except for the heretic Marcion, who rejected much of the New Testament. (3) If Paul did not write this letter, then it was the work of someone as great or even greater than Paul. No such person is known to us.

The Contents of Ephesians. Like most of Paul's letters, this one has two major parts: Part 1 is doctrinal (1:3–3:21); and Part 2 is practical (4:1–6:20). The major theme of the doctrinal section is unity. The development of the argument seems to be based on the unity of creation, when God viewed creation "and behold, it was very good." According to this letter, the purpose of God is to restore this pristine unity in Christ through the church. Christ is the principle of unity, and the church is the means.

Outline of Ephesians

Part 1. Christ, the principle of unity (1:3–3:21)
   a. Christ is the means of election, adoption, redemption, and forgiveness (1:4-7).
   b. All things are summed up in Christ (1:10).
   c. All things are subject to Christ (1:22).
   d. Resurrection and exaltation of the believer are through Christ (2:6).
   e. Reconciliation is possible only through Christ (2:16).
   f. God's eternal purpose for humanity is fulfilled in Christ (3:6).

Part 2. The church, the means of unity (4:1–6:20)
   a. The unity of the church is like the unity in the human body (4:1-16).
   b. This unity in the church will affect all of humankind (4:17–6:20).

THE LETTER TO THE COLOSSIANS

Theme: Full Salvation in Christ

Paul's letter to the Colossians is an important one; at the same time, it is possibly the most difficult of his letters to understand. It is of special importance because it deals profoundly with the person and work of Christ (Colossians 1:12-20). It is difficult because it refers—occasionally in technical terms, but more often by allusion—to a heresy in the Colossian church that is nowhere clearly defined.

The Origin and Character of the Colossian Church. Apparently Paul himself had never visited Colossae (1:4; 2:1), though it is likely that the establishment of the church was a direct result of his long ministry in Ephesus. The founder and possible pastor of the church may have been Epaphras, who is mentioned prominently in this letter (1:7; 4:12-13).

The city of Colossae lies about 100 miles east of Ephesus in what was formerly the kingdom of Phrygia. Being on the main road from the Euphrates to Ephesus, it was exposed not only to local Greek and Phrygian influences but also to the many strange cults coming from the Orient. Nearly two hundred years before the composition of this letter, two thousand Jewish families had been imported from Babylon and settled in this area, so that by New Testament times Judaism was deeply rooted there and had become very influential.

Why Did Paul Write a Letter of This Character? The concluding verses of Acts (Acts 28:17-31) suggest that Paul continued to give active direction to his far-flung missionary work all through his two-year imprisonment at Rome. Among the many persons who visited Paul during this period was Epaphras. He brought Paul encouraging reports of the growth of the work of Christ at Colossae and in the nearby cities of Laodicea and Hierapolis; but at the same time he brought disquieting news of the growth of non-Christian tendencies which, if allowed to develop, might have destroyed those things that are at the very heart of the gospel. In the Colossian church there were apparently some broad-minded individuals who felt that the preaching of salvation by grace through faith alone was not enough, and that to this gospel should be added certain Jewish and pagan elements. Both Epaphras and Paul saw that such a tendency, if tolerated, would ultimately lead these believers once again into bondage to legalism, taboo, ritualism, and superstition. It was primarily to combat such a tendency that Paul wrote this epistle.

It is not necessary to decide whether this heretical tendency was basically Jewish or Gentile; it was both, mixed with elements of Christianity into a kind of theological "tossed salad." If we assume—though not all scholars would agree—that the basic ingredient added to the gospel was Judaism, this does not mean that the problems of the Galatian church (compare chapter 3) were being repeated at Colossae. At Galatia the Judaizers were seeking to add to the gospel certain elements of pure Jewish legalism, which was dangerous enough; but in Colossae not even the Jewish elements were undefiled. Frederick F. Bruce refers to a Talmudic saying to the effect that Phrygian wine and baths had separated the ten tribes from their fellow Israelites.[6] Furthermore an ancient inscription from this region tells of a Jewish woman who was both honorary ruler of the synagogue and priestess of the imperial cult![7] Broad-mindedness indeed!

In this Hellenistic type of Judaism, it appears that an exalted place was given to angelic beings. In Jewish teaching, it was through angels that the law was given (see Hebrews 2:2), and the apocryphal books of Enoch and Testaments of the XII Patriarchs exhibit an elaborate angelic hierarchy. Since several of the popular oriental cults—often carelessly called Gnostic—also taught that an array of cosmic spirits separated the pure god from impure human beings, it was a simple matter to combine the Jewish and pagan respect for angels into a cult of angel worship (compare Colossians 1:16; 2:8-10, 15, 18, 20-23).

The Gentile influence shows itself especially in an emphasis on the importance of knowledge as an aid to salvation. In this connection Paul warns them against "philosophy and empty deceit" (2:8), using such words as "fullness" (1:19), "knowledge" (1:9; 2:3), and "severity to the body" (2:23). All of these terms are found frequently in the Gnostic literature of the second and third centuries, and their presence in this epistle suggests that they were technical terms even in Paul's day. These Gentile groups apparently thought that the work of Christ by itself was imperfect and needed to be supplemented by mystic knowledge *(gnosis)* and rigorous discipline of the body (asceticism) so that earthbound human beings could escape the influence of the vast spiritual forces of the cosmos arrayed against them (2:15, 20).

How Did Paul Deal with This Problem? In his letter to the Galatians, Paul had been angry with the Judaizers and impatient with those who had been misled by them. In contrast, the tone of Colossians is calm and measured, as though Paul understood fully the insidious nature of their temptations and appreciated their struggle to overcome them. His attack is directed first at the "theological problem," as it concerned the person of Christ, and next at the "practical problem" created by this heresy in the lives of the believers.

Conceivably, Paul might have attempted to destroy this dangerous tendency by attacking its practices or its leaders, but instead his strategy was to present such an exalted picture of Christ that, by contrast, they would recognize the limitations of their own system and abandon it. Christ is presented as absolutely preeminent, the very center of the universe, ruler of all cosmic powers. He is the image and fullness of God, and by his incarnate work he is the Head of the church, which in its work is to be the continuation of his incarnation.

In practical matters, Paul attacks those efforts that sought to add other elements to the finished work of Christ. He shows that all such efforts are merely evidences of human pride. Certainly the Christian must seek to put away evil practices and put on the new person (3:10), but these may be achieved only on the basis of faith in Christ through the indwelling Spirit.

THE LETTER TO PHILEMON

Theme: Onesimus, a Brother Beloved

No serious question has ever been raised about the authorship of this charming letter. In spite of its brevity, it breathes in every phrase the mind and spirit of Paul, and since it is quite personal, it gives the reader a rare opportunity to see Paul the man.

The Purpose of the Letter. Some interpreters have seen in this letter an allegory in which, as Luther said, "We are all Onesimuses," slaves of sin for whom Christ pleads that God may be gracious and forego our rightful punishment. The most widely accepted view, however, is that Paul is addressing a plea to Philemon for the forgiveness and acceptance of Onesimus, a runaway slave. John Knox has argued for a different purpose for this letter (see *The Interpreter's Bible,* Vol. XII, or his book, *Philemon Among the Letters of Paul*).

Philemon, apparently, was a wealthy resident of Colossae, and it was in his home that the church usually met. It is assumed by many that Apphia was his wife and Archippus his son. The letter suggests that Onesimus had not only run away, but also had robbed his master before leaving. Somehow he came to Rome and, finding himself destitute, appealed for help to Paul, his former master's friend. While Onesimus stayed with Paul, he was converted and became so useful to Paul that Paul gave him a new name, "Mr. Helpful" (Greek, Onesimus, vv. 10-11).

It was a serious crime for a slave to run away, and it was an equally serious offense for a Christian slave not to return. So it was necessary for Onesimus to return and for Paul to plead for his acceptance. Paul bases his plea on four points: (1) he is himself a prisoner for Christ, verse 9; (2) Onesimus is Paul's spiritual child, verse 10; (3) Onesimus is greatly loved, "My very heart," verse 12; (4) Philemon is in spiritual debt to Paul, verse 19. The very fact that this letter was preserved suggests strongly that Paul's plea was effective.

THE LETTER TO THE PHILIPPIANS

Theme: Joy in the Lord

The Church at Philippi appears to have been without serious problems, and there are few serious critical problems in connection with this epistle. Little question has been raised about the Pauline authorship. The date seems to be about A.D. 60, and the place of writing Rome, though recently some have argued for Caesarea or Ephesus.

Why Did Paul Write This Letter? This epistle is not concerned with one dominant theme, but rather with the general concern of pastor for flock. One of its delightful characteristics is the informal, almost casual, way in which the author moves from theme to theme, seeing in each the goodness of God and a reason for rejoicing.

The particular occasion for the writing of the letter appears to be the return of Epaphroditus to Philippi. Paul intends to send Timothy there to minister to them (2:19-23) and shortly thereafter to come himself (2:24). According to Philippians 2:25, the church had sent Paul a gift by the hands of Epaphroditus, who stayed in Rome to minister to the apostle. During this period, Epaphroditus had become ill (perhaps with the dreaded "marsh fever" or malaria) and had nearly died (2:27). The Philippians, hearing of his illness, were greatly concerned, and Epaphroditus himself longed to be home once again. Paul, therefore, decided to send him home as the bearer of this letter which is a kind of "certificate of Christian merit."

If this is the main theme, a secondary one appears in chapter 4:10-20. Here Paul delicately balances two important principles: (1) his need for and appreciation of the gift from Philippi (4:10, 14-16, 18); (2) his absolute faith in the providence of God (4:11-13, 17-20). Paul wishes to encourage the churches to assume responsibility for mission support, but at the same time he asserts his independence of the churches and his complete trust in the Lord.

The Kenosis ("Self-emptying") Passage. Undoubtedly, the most unique theological passage is that found in Philippians 2:1-11. No brief discussion can possibly do justice to it. Here we can do only two things: (1) clarify the context, and (2) suggest the major points that Paul emphasizes.

The context of this significant passage is a plea for unity and humility in the Christian community. As a basis for this plea, Christ is presented as the supreme example of humility (2:5-11). Paul's argument is built around three points: (1) the preexistent status of Christ as in the form of God (2:5-6); (2) the self-humiliation of Christ to the status of a servant suffering death upon a cross (2:7-8); (3) the exaltation of Christ to the place of supreme honor (2:9-11).

With Christ as the example, the Philippians are urged to "work out" their salvation (received by grace through faith) until it dominates all of life (2:9-11).

- Why did Paul attach such great importance to the collection he was taking for the poor at Jerusalem? How does it compare to our United Way or similar appeals?
- Why were heretical tendencies likely to develop in Colossae? How do our present cities compare with that situation?
- Why would it have been difficult for Paul to oppose openly the institution of slavery in his letter to Philemon? How does this letter influence our thinking about race relations?

Additional Resources

Bruce, Frederick F., *The Epistle to the Ephesians.* Westwood, N.J.: Fleming H. Revell, 1962.

Mitton, C. Leslie, *Ephesians.* Grand Rapids, Mich.: William B. Eerdmans Publishing Co., 1976.

Edward Schweizer, *The Letter to the Colossians.* Minneapolis: Augsburg Publishing Co., 1982.

6

THE STORY OF JESUS IS
PUT IN WRITING

Matthew, Mark, Luke-Acts

Life always precedes literature. First, there was the Living Word, who was himself the embodiment of God's redemptive love and the agent of its first proclamation to the world; next came the written word, composed by inspired believers, through whom Jesus continued to act and to speak.

By the sixth decade of the first century, even though the church had carried the gospel "unto the uttermost part" of the Roman world, there was concern that, when the authentic voice of the apostles was heard no more, the church itself would cease to be. It became urgent, therefore, to enshrine in written form the story of Jesus that all ages might hear and be saved.

What Are the Gospels? It may be helpful to approach an answer to this question by looking first at several erroneous suggestions.

1. The Gospels, whether considered individually or collectively, are not the life of Christ. Though in large part biographical, the writers never intended them to be complete biographies. For example: Mark tells us nothing about the Nativity or the early Judean ministry, few of the parables, and almost nothing of the post-resurrection events. Matthew and Luke give different accounts of the Nativity, different genealogies, and often different settings for what appear to be the same teachings.

2. The Gospels were not intended to be literary works. Though in some parts they exhibit good literary form and show remarkable beauty, for the most part they are written in the rough, colloquial Greek common to the Mediterranean world of that day.

3. The Gospels are not theological treatises. Though they are

thoroughly theological in character, they present a theology in life, rather than in proposition.

What then, are the Gospels? The simplest answer is that they are a written form of the apostolic preaching. This answer, however, is not entirely adequate, for nearly a generation of Christian preaching had passed by before the first Gospel appeared. They represent more than the preaching of any one apostle, or of all the apostles; they are documents intended primarily for the church in its work of evangelism and missions, its instruction of converts, its training in Christian living, and its defense against pagan philosophies. Avery Dulles has put the matter admirably:

> As confessional documents, the Gospels speak only to potential or actual believers. They contain nothing to satisfy the imagination of the novelist or the curiosity of the chronicler. They do not present Jesus "according to the flesh," but as seen in the light of the Spirit. Only to the man who is earnestly seeking communion with God will the Gospels yield their full message.[8]

THE INTERRELATIONSHIP OF
THE SYNOPTIC GOSPELS

The Synoptic Gospels are those by Matthew, Mark, and Luke; they are called "synoptic" because they present a common synopsis of the life and words of Jesus. The Fourth Gospel has a different purpose and consequently a different form. Anyone who uses a harmony of the Gospels, where similar material is arranged in parallel columns, will be immediately impressed with the great similarity of the accounts given in the first three Gospels. Since we assume that the Synoptic Gospels were written by three different authors, we are forced to ask why they are so much alike, and also why, in certain places, they are so different. To say that they are alike "because that is the way things happened" is not a satisfying reply, because all three Gospels (omitting duplications) record only about as many words of Jesus as the average minister uses in three sermons and no more events than would fill a busy month. This is a mere fragment from a busy ministry of more than two years! Quite obviously, the Gospel writers were selective (Luke 1:1-4; John 20:30-31; 21:25). But why, out of the enormous volume

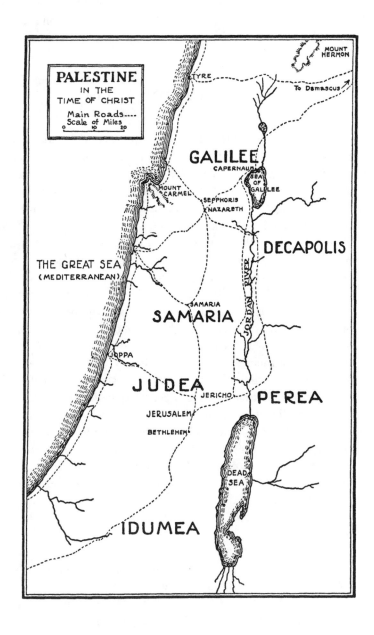

PALESTINE
IN THE
TIME OF CHRIST
Main Roads----
Scale of Miles
0   10   20

MOUNT HERMON

TYRE

To Damascus

GALILEE
CAPERNAUM
SEA OF GALILEE

MOUNT CARMEL

SEPPHORIS
NAZARETH

DECAPOLIS

THE GREAT SEA
(MEDITERRANEAN)

SAMARIA
SAMARIA

JORDAN RIVER

JOPPA

JUDEA
JERICHO
PEREA
JERUSALEM
BETHLEHEM

DEAD SEA

IDUMEA

of Jesus' teaching and the multitudinous events of his crowded life, did they select almost the same events and relate them in the same order, often in identical language? This question is known as the Synoptic Problem.

SUGGESTED SOLUTIONS OF
THE SYNOPTIC PROBLEM

Early Attempts. This problem did not suddenly arise out of nineteenth-century German scholarship, but was recognized even by some of the very early church authorities. One of the earliest suggested solutions was that Matthew's Gospel, in Hebrew, was the first to be written. It was then assumed that Matthew was known and used by Mark and Luke and that the differences that occur grew out of the varying aims of the authors and out of their different ways of translating the same Hebrew original. For various reasons this theory was soon abandoned, although some scholars (mostly Catholic) still hold to the view that Matthew was first.

A more widely accepted theory was that the oral gospel (see chapter 2) became fixed in form by the middle of the first century and that the similarities in the Gospels can be explained by assuming that all of them were based on this common oral gospel. This theory that a commonly accepted oral gospel existed before the advent of the written Gospels is generally believed today. It also is admitted that this oral gospel probably had assumed a rather fixed form, but few scholars believe that this theory can account for the minute linguistic similarities among the Synoptics, where even a parenthesis (Matthew 9:6; Mark 2:10; Luke 5:24) is common to all three. A documentary relationship appears to be the most satisfactory explanation.

The Two-Document Theory. The basic assumptions of this theory are:

1. The earliest Gospel is that by Mark. (See the section on Mark for the reasons for this belief.)
2. Mark's Gospel was freely used by both Matthew and Luke.
3. Matthew and Luke also made considerable use of another document (now lost) that consisted largely of sayings of

Jesus. For convenience, this lost document is called "Q" (German *Quelle* or "source").

Some people are troubled by any suggestion that the writers of the New Testament used "sources"; they feel that this is in some way a denial of inspiration. In this connection it will be helpful to read Luke 1:1-4, where Luke clearly states that he knew of other sources and made use of them; yet he also believed that he wrote in accord with the will of God.

What, then, is the evidence presented for this two-document solution of the problem? If we assume that the earliest Gospel was Mark's, these points may be noted:

1. *The Subject Matter.* Matthew and Luke include most of Mark's subject matter. The best Greek text of Mark contains 661 verses. Of these, at least 610 are found in Matthew and Luke. Of the eighty-three separate paragraphs in Mark, *only three* are absent from the other Synoptics (Mark 4:26-29; 7:32-37; 8:22-26).

2. *The Identical Language.* Matthew and Luke often repeat the exact words of Mark. This is true of 51 percent of Matthew and 53 percent of Luke.

3. *The Common Order of Events.* Since so few of the events in the life of our Lord are recorded in the Gospels, it is rather remarkable to find that Matthew and Luke so largely follow Mark's order, and even though one or the other may depart from it, they never unite against Mark in this regard.

Evidence for the Use of Another Document. There are not only remarkable similarities among the Synoptic Gospels, but also equally remarkable differences. Most of these differences are in the inclusion or omission of sayings of Jesus; that is, "Q."

1. Both Matthew and Luke contain many verses not found in Mark, and they have over two hundred of these in common.

2. Papias (c. A.D. 140) refers to a book of sayings of Jesus: "Matthew compiled the *logia,* oracles or sayings in the Hebrew [Aramaic?] language and everyone translated them as he was able" (see the section on Matthew).

3. The recently discovered Gospel According to Thomas, which consists entirely of sayings attributed to Jesus, gives further evidence that such documents were in circulation.

All of this—though short of proof that such a document as "Q" was used by Matthew and Luke—indicates a strong probability in that direction.

Were other documents used besides Mark and "Q"? Luke 1:1-4, seems to imply that Luke had access to many sources, oral and written. After we have marked off those verses in Matthew and Luke that seem to be based on Mark and "Q," there are left more than three hundred verses that are peculiar to Matthew, and more than four hundred that are found only in Luke. Presumably these come from other sources or, in the case of Matthew, from his own recollections. Matthew's special sources are usually called "M" and Luke's, "L."

A diagram may help to simplify this rather complex problem.

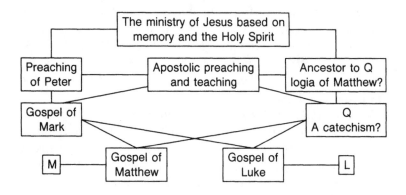

THE GOSPEL ACCORDING TO MARK

The order of the Gospels, as found in the ancient manuscripts, is not always that which we have in our modern Bibles—Matthew, Mark, Luke, John. The reason for the arrangement is usually not given, though it probably was influenced to some degree by the popularity of a particular Gospel in the area from which the manuscript originated. Since most scholars agree that Mark was written first, we shall begin with this Gospel.

The Writer and His Readers. While Mark was not one of the original Twelve, he was closely associated with the work of Paul, of Barnabas, and—if tradition is to be trusted—with Peter during

Peter's residence at Rome. It was the unanimous belief of early historians that this Gospel was written by the John Mark mentioned in the New Testament (Acts 12:12, 25; 15:39; 2 Timothy 4:11; and probably Mark 14:51).

The earliest mention of Mark as the author is to be found in the *Church History* of Eusebius (3:39) where Eusebius quotes Papias, who lived in the early part of the second century: "Mark, having become the interpreter of Peter, wrote down accurately everything that he remembered without, however, recording in order what was either said or done by Christ."

Later in the same century (A.D. 160–180), the *Anti-Marcionite Prologues to the Gospels* contributed this statement: "Mark was Peter's interpreter, and after Peter's decease wrote down this same Gospel in the region of Italy."

About A.D. 180, Irenaeus also attested to the Markan authorship.

When and Where Was the Gospel Written? According to tradition, the later years of Peter's life were spent in Rome, and there is nothing improbable in the tradition that Mark was with him. There is some evidence from Mark's occasional use of Latin words (*centurio, speculator, legio, denarius,* and so forth) that he wrote largely for Christians living in or near Rome. His Gospel, in oral form, may have taken shape during his early teaching experience as the companion of Paul and Barnabas (A.D. 50–55), been put in writing during his sojourn in Italy, and been published after Peter's death. Such a theory would not only satisfy the requirement for an early date of composition, which seems to be required by the primitive character of the Gospel, but also satisfy the statement of Irenaeus that it was written (published?) after Peter's death. According to this theory, we may suggest that the Gospel was completed and published about A.D. 65, having been based upon an oral Gospel developed and used in the instruction of missionary converts as early as A.D. 50–55.

The Major Critical Problem. This has to do with the ending (Mark 16:9-20). The problem is complicated, and no suggested solution is accepted by all. Many of the oldest and best manuscripts end at 16:8 or else have a conclusion different from the so-called "longer ending" found in the text of the King James

Version. For many years it was assumed that the original ending of Mark's Gospel had been lost and that some scribe or scribes, during its early history, had supplied another ending derived from Matthew and Luke. In more recent days some notable scholars have insisted that Mark meant to end his Gospel abruptly and on a note of awe with the statement "and they were afraid" (16:8). This is one of the continuing problems for which textual scholars are seeking a solution. Though it is a matter of importance that we discover, if possible, the correct ending, no doctrinal matter seems to be involved, and the problem in no way weakens the authority of the book.

Characteristics of Mark's Gospel. (1) It has all the vividness and authenticity of an eyewitness report and suggests the viewpoint of Peter. (2) It emphasizes the humanity of Jesus, but never at the expense of his uniqueness as the Son of God. (3) It is full of color and movement, as though seen by an active man of the outdoors. The word "straightway" is used approximately twenty times in the King James Version.

The Plan of the Gospel. The key to an understanding of this Gospel is this: though Jesus knew himself from the very first to be the Messiah, he chose to hide that fact until near the end of his ministry, when its true meaning could be understood.

Aside from a brief introduction and conclusion, the Gospel falls into two main divisions:

1. The ministry in Galilee (chapters 1–9)
   Transition: the journey to Jerusalem (chapter 10)
2. The Last Week in Jerusalem (chapters 11–16)

THE GOSPEL ACCORDING TO MATTHEW

As has been stated previously, no order of the Gospels is common to all of the ancient manuscripts. Nevertheless, Matthew's Gospel appears to have been the most widely read and the most often quoted. Reasons for this are not hard to find: (1) It gives the most complete record of our Lord's teachings and does this without sacrificing the main substance of the narrative of his life and work. (2) Much of the material is arranged topically, which makes it easy to use in teaching. (3) It reflects most clearly the Jewish environment in which Jesus lived and taught. (4) It links together most effectively the Old Testament with the New Testament.

The Writer and His Readers. The earliest clue we have to the writer of this Gospel is found in the writings of Papias, mentioned earlier in this chapter. The general tradition of the church has attributed the writing of this Gospel to Levi, also known as Matthew the son of Alphaeus (Matthew 9:9; 10:3; Mark 2:14; 3:18; Luke 5:27-29; 6:15; Acts 1:13). According to tradition, not long after the ascension, Matthew wrote a brief Aramaic account of the most important teachings of Jesus. During the fifteen years in which he worked in Palestine, he used his brief Gospel (perhaps the *logia* of which Papias speaks) written in the vernacular of that land. Later, says this same tradition, he moved his field of service to Syria and worked in or near Antioch. Since Greek was more commonly spoken in that area, he may have rewritten his Aramaic Gospel, possibly with the help of one or more Christian associates, in the Greek language and enlarged it to include material from Mark's Gospel and other sources.

This theory appears to meet the two major objections to Matthew's authorship raised by many modern scholars: (1) The Gospel of Matthew, as we now have it, does not appear to be a translation, but a work originally composed in Greek. (2) It is difficult to understand how Matthew, one of the original Twelve, would depend on so much of the work of Mark, who was not an apostle. Most of the arguments for and against the Matthaean authorship are based on either conjecture or tradition. This much, however, is based on fact: witness to the traditional authorship of Matthew is strong, clear, and consistent in the early church, and no argument that is decisive has yet been advanced against the reliability of this tradition. Matthew's Gospel undoubtedly was written for Jewish readers in Palestine and beyond.

When and Where Was It Written? Antioch in Syria has the best claim as the place of writing. If, as has been suggested, Matthew's Gospel appeared in an Aramaic "first edition," this may have been composed as early as A.D. 60–65, and the Greek form of the Gospel written ten or fifteen years later.

The Aim and Plan of the Gospel. The central message is that Jesus is the fulfillment of Jewish prophecy. Its aim seems to be to supplement Mark's Gospel with more of the teachings of Jesus and to arrange the material in such a way that it might be easily and effectively used by Christian teachers and apologists. One scholar, R. G. V. Tasker, has noted that the arrangement of the material shows that Matthew thought of his Gospel as the "Christian Pentateuch" for the New Israel. Tasker continues: "Just as there were five books of the old Jewish law—the Pentateuch—so the Evangelist groups the sayings of Jesus in five books, each of which is concluded by much the same formula: 'And it came to pass, when Jesus had finished these sayings' (7:28; 11:1; 13:53; 19:1; 26:1)."[9] These five books are:

1. The Sermon on the Mount (chapters 5–7)
2. The Appointment and Missionary Work of the Twelve (chapter 10)
3. The Parables of the Kingdom (chapter 13)
4. The Conduct of Believers in the Christian Community (chapter 18)
5. The Teachings of Jesus on Last Things (chapters 24–25)

THE GOSPEL ACCORDING TO LUKE

It is impossible to write of the Gospel of Luke without, at the same time, referring to Luke's second volume, The Acts of the Apostles. In the three preceding chapters, the Epistles of Paul were presented in the context of Paul's missionary journeys, as related by Luke in the Acts. It will not be necessary to review these, but in our study of the Gospel of Luke we must continually keep in mind that it is volume one of a two-volume work, even though the second volume (Acts) is not a continuation of the Gospel form, but a travel narrative telling of the spread of the gospel from Jerusalem to Rome.

The Writer and His Readers. It is generally agreed that whoever wrote the Gospel wrote the Acts also, and there seems to be no good reason to question the unanimous tradition of the early church that this writer was Luke, "the beloved physician," who was a companion of Paul. Since one of the most important considerations for admission of a book to the canon (to be discussed in Chapter 10) was apostolic authorship, and since Luke was not an apostle, it seems quite unlikely that he would have been named as author of these books if the early church had entertained any doubt about the matter. Furthermore, the author of these two books was known to Theophilus (Luke 1:3; Acts 1:1) and also to Paul, as is shown by the "we" passages (Acts 16:10-17; 20:5-16; 21:1-18; 27:1–28:16). To be sure, there were other companions of Paul, but out of the very limited number of regular followers— Titus, Justus, Crescens, and Luke—Luke alone seems qualified to be the author of these two books.

Though both of the books are dedicated to a notable Christian named Theophilus, they undoubtedly were intended for a wider audience. From a study of the books themselves, it seems clear that the audience was made up chiefly of Gentiles, Hellenistic Jews, or both. Luke is careful to explain, for their benefit, geographical details of Palestine and to avoid puzzling Semitic words, such as *rabbi* or *hosanna* and obscure Jewish allusions such as "abomination of desolation" (compare Matthew 24:15 and Mark 13:14 with Luke 21:20). Furthermore Luke does not conclude his genealogy of Jesus with Abraham (see Matthew 1:2), but carries it back through Adam to God, thus including the Gentiles (Luke 3:38).

Date and Place of Writing. Since Luke was a companion of Paul during his imprisonment in Caesarea, it seems quite likely that he began to write the Gospel at that time (c. A.D. 58–60), though publication probably was delayed for some time. During his stay in Palestine, Luke had access not only to other "narratives," both oral and written (Luke 1:1), but also to living eyewitnesses, including certain of the apostles (compare "ministers of the word," Luke 1:2), and possibly even Mary herself. The "we" sections of the Acts suggest that Luke kept a diary during his missionary work with Paul, and it seems likely that some portions of the Acts may have been written before the Gospel. With regard to the dating of both books, one of the principal questions has to do with their relation to the fall of Jerusalem (A.D. 70). Able scholars argue that Luke must have known of the attack on Jerusalem before he wrote the Gospel, and they cite Luke 21:20 as an indication of this. Other scholars, equally able, present strong arguments in favor of a date prior to A.D. 70. Since there is no complete agreement at present, it seems unwise to abandon the traditional dates of about A.D. 65 for the Gospel and about A.D. 68 for the Acts, which are based on the assumption that Paul was released from his first Roman imprisonment before the Neronian persecution and was later rearrested and martyred about A.D. 68 or 69.

The Plan of the Gospel. Luke's Gospel falls naturally into five parts:

1. The Nativity and childhood of Jesus (chapters 1–2)
2. The beginning of Jesus' public ministry (3:1–4:13)
3. The great Galilean ministry (4:14–9:50)
4. From Galilee to Jerusalem (9:51–19:48)
5. Last public ministry in Jerusalem; crucifixion, resurrection (chapters 20–24)

The Purpose and Plan of the Acts. The Acts is more than a mere travel narrative. Luke seems to have had a desire to convince the Roman authorities through this narrative that the new religion was no threat to their government; a second purpose, no less important, seems to have been to help overcome suspicions and conflict between Jewish and Gentile Christians. This latter aim seems confirmed by the plan of the book. Of the twenty-eight chapters, the first twelve deal largely with Jewish Christianity, with Peter as the leading figure. The remaining chapters (13–28) tell the story of the Gentile mission, with Paul as the outstanding character. Luke takes pains to show the debt of Gentile Christianity to the Palestinian church, and through the collection for the poor in Jerusalem the mission churches show their recognition of this obligation.

- What was the general aim of the Gospels and how do they apply to our situation today?
- Assuming that the Gospel writers used human sources, how does this idea affect your belief in inspiration?
- What is the importance of information regarding the authorship, dates, and sources for the Gospels?
- What do the Gospels tell us about the "historical Jesus"?

Additional Resources

Dodd, C. H., *The Parables of the Kingdom.* New York: Harper & Row, Publishers, Inc., 1981.

Hunter, Archibald M., *A Pattern for Life: An Exposition of the Sermon on the Mount.* Philadelphia: The Westminster Press, 1966.

Hunter, Archibald M., *Introducing the New Testament.* rev. ed. Philadelphia: The Westminster Press, 1958.

7

ORGANIZATION AND THOUGHT
IN A MATURING CHURCH

The Pastoral Epistles and Hebrews

It is incorrect to speak, as some do, of "the organization of the first-century church" or of "first-century theology" as though they were fixed entities. During the first century, both the organization and the theology of the church were living things, and, as with all living things, they were subject to growth. The Pastoral Epistles—First and Second Timothy and Titus—illustrate most clearly this flexibility and growth in organization, and the Epistle to the Hebrews is a good example of the changing form of theological expression as the early church sought to bring the gospel to the Greek as well as to the Hebrew mind.

THE PASTORAL EPISTLES

The term "Pastoral Epistles" is nowhere found in the New Testament, nor does it fully describe the nature of the letters to Timothy and Titus, but since the term is well known, it is a convenient label for these epistles. Nearly all of the New Testament letters are "pastoral" in that they were written by missionary pastors and contain much pastoral counsel. The so-called Pastoral Epistles—especially First Timothy and Titus—are unique, however, in the large proportion of space given to matters of ecclesiastical organization and activity.

The Earliest Forms of Church Organization. Although Jesus seems to have given no directions for the organization of the church (the word "church" is found only twice in the Gospels; see Matthew 16:18 and 18:17), the outlines for such organization seem to be implicit both in Jesus' teachings and in his actions. In the first place, Jesus himself declared his intention to establish a church (Matthew 16:18), and by the appointment of the Twelve he took the first steps toward its organization. Second, Jesus and his disciples continued their association with the synagogue, which served as a pattern for the earliest churches. Here, then, were the two basic characteristics of early church organization: (1) the *apostolate,* with its general responsibility for the "ministry of the word" (Acts 6:4), and (2) the *synagogue,* with an organization consisting of a "ruler" (Acts 18:8) and a board of elders. All other forms of organization appear to have developed from this simple pattern in response to particular needs (Acts 6:1-6). For the sake of simplicity, we may think of the earliest churches as "Christian synagogues" in which the apostolate was somewhat analogous to the Sanhedrin, the local bishops (pastors) corresponded somewhat to the ruler of the synagogue, and the presbyters (elders) were similar to the board of elders responsible for the ongoing operation of the synagogue.

Why a More Elaborate Organization Was Needed. While we do not know all the reasons, three can be mentioned:

1. *The number of the churches was increasing.* It is impossible to say how many Christian congregations, independent of the Jewish synagogues, were in existence before the fall of Jerusalem in A.D. 70. But we may assume that early tradition is not entirely in error when it narrates the labors of other members of the apostolate in much the same terms as those used by Luke in telling of the missionary activities of Peter and Paul. It is altogether possible that within a generation after the ascension there were several hundred churches scattered throughout the Roman world. Greater numbers demanded more organization.

2. *The character of the churches was changing.* One might argue that numbers alone would not necessarily require a more elaborate form of ecclesiastical organization so long as the general constituency remained rather constant. Yet, not only were there more churches, but they were becoming less Jewish in character. The traditional ties of common history and language were becoming less significant. Such a change brought with it the seeds of misun-

derstanding and discord, echoes of which may be heard throughout the Acts and the Epistles.

3. *The environment of the church was changing.* The world of the church before Paul's missionary journeys was largely Jewish, and in it Christians—in spite of occasional persecution—probably found acceptance by their Jewish neighbors. This attitude of acceptance depended largely on the stability of life under the Romans, and this began to change after the death of Augustus (A.D. 14). The impact of this was not felt immediately, but as political conditions in the Empire grew more chaotic, the suspicious attitude toward Christians, by both Jews and Romans, changed into open persecution. This general instability affected the traditional religions, both Jewish and pagan, and there was a general tendency toward inclusivism or irreligion. The inevitable reaction of the leaders of the Christian churches was one of increased emphasis on church organization and leadership, which became the major theme of the Pastoral Epistles.

Did Paul Write the Pastoral Epistles? Until the rise of the modern scientific study of the New Testament, this question of Paul's authorship of the Pastoral Epistles seems never to have been raised. Toward the end of the second century Irenaeus asserted that Paul wrote them. In the early third century Tertullian and Clement of Alexandria added their confirmation to the general acceptance of the early church. Since all three of these books claim that Paul was the author, it becomes important to seek for the reasons for questioning this strong, early attestation. The objections that certain scholars have raised are as follows:

1. The history implied in these letters seems difficult to reconcile with the framework of Paul's life as given by Luke in the Acts. In rebuttal, other scholars have pointed out that Luke does not claim to tell all that Paul did, and the early patristic tradition speaks of missionary work after the first Roman imprisonment (see Eusebius). Clement of Rome declares that Paul went to "the extremity of the west," which in those days meant Spain. None of this is mentioned by Luke.

2. Some believe that the church organization in the Pastorals is too advanced for Paul's day. Others, reading the same material, are equally convinced that the Pastoral Epistles present a relatively

simple church structure and that only by "reading in" ideas from a later date can one see second-century forms.

3. Another objection raised is that the heresies attacked in the Pastoral Epistles belong to a period later than the lifetime of Paul. To a large extent this argument has been silenced by the discovery of the Dead Sea Scrolls and the Gnostic literature from Nag Hammadi. It is clear from this material that the heresies noted in these epistles antedated the Christian era and in all probability had grown into dangerous movements by the sixth decade of the first century.

4. The most serious objection against Pauline authorship grows out of a diligent study of the style and language, which admittedly are quite different from that found in the other letters of Paul. About one-third of the words used are absent from Paul's other letters, and, to add to the difficulty, certain other key words appear to have acquired a new meaning. Lack of space forbids a full discussion of these objections, but advocates of Pauline authorship point out the following: (1) These letters have a different purpose from Paul's other letters; hence new words were necessary. (2) Paul was older, and both age and added experience had wrought changes in him. (3) The new problems made necessary changes in the meaning of certain words. (4) As Paul grew older he may have depended more on his assistants in the writing of his missionary letters, even to the extent of allowing them freedom in composition while he acted as general editor.

First Timothy. This letter probably was written after Paul's release from his first Roman imprisonment. He had placed Timothy at Ephesus as his apostolic deputy. While Timothy held this important and difficult post at a time when rapid changes were taking place, Paul wrote to his deputy and through him to the churches of that area. First, he urged Timothy to deal effectively with certain teachers who were spreading false ideas both of the law and of the gospel (chapter 1). Next, he called upon the church to have universal concern in its prayer life, and he urged modesty in conduct, especially in the demeanor of women (chapter 2). He then outlined certain qualifications for church officers (chapter 3). Chapter 4 has to do largely with ideals for Timothy's own private and public life. In chapter 5, Paul deals with the treatment of various groups in the church, especially the elderly and the widows. Finally, the letter gives directions concerning slaves, false teachers, and the rich (chapter 6).

Titus. The letter to Titus probably preceded the second letter to Timothy. Little is known of Titus, and there is no mention of his name in the Acts, but apparently he was one of Paul's most trusted assistants. He had preached in Dalmatia (2 Timothy 4:10), and when this letter was written he was engaged in the evangelization of Crete. Since the needs of the church were similar, one would expect that much of Paul's advice in 1 Timothy would be found also in Titus, and this is the case. Chapter 1 deals with the qualifications of church officers and attitudes toward Judaizers. Chapter 2 is quite similar to 1 Timothy 5, whereas the third and final chapter stresses the importance of Christian attitudes.

Second Timothy. This letter is less pastoral and more personal than the others. It breathes an atmosphere of deep affection for Timothy (chapter 1) and a conviction that he will remain faithful even when others prove untrue (chapter 2). Certain warnings (given in 1 Timothy) are repeated (chapter 3), and the letter closes with a final charge to "preach the word" and rejoin Paul as soon as possible (chapter 4).

THE EPISTLE TO THE HEBREWS

William Barclay aptly calls this: "The letter which would not be denied,"[10] for, though it is quoted with approval by Clement of Rome as early as A.D. 95 and was read in many of the early churches, it did not find a secure place in the canon (the authoritative collection of New Testament books) until the fourth century. There seems to have been almost unanimous agreement from the late first century onward that the authentic note of the inspired word could be heard in this epistle. Yet the church hesitated to include it in the canon. The reason seems clear: The church knew nothing of its author. Since the primary purpose of the canon was to collect the writings of the apostles, and since there was no tradition of apostolic authorship for Hebrews, the church hesitated for nearly two centuries before accepting Hebrews into the canon. It did so finally, not because it had at long last discovered that it was apostolic, but because of the intrinsic worth of the epistle. So convincingly did it speak of Christ that it "would not be denied" a place of authority.

Early Attitudes Toward Authorship. Concerning the authorship of this book, three attitudes developed, one connected with each of the three major branches of the early church.

1. The Eastern Church, centered at Alexandria in Egypt, decided quite early that the writer was Paul. Since these Alexandrian Christians were well versed in the Greek language, they were well aware of the great differences between the Greek of this epistle and that found in other known correspondence of Paul. But they came to believe that Paul had written it in the Hebrew language and that it had then been translated by some Greek-speaking person like Luke (or Clement of Alexandria), or by some unknown disciple whose identity, Origen said, "God only knows for certain."

2. The North African churches took a position directly opposite to that of the Eastern churches; they rejected Paul as the author and attributed the letter to some other person. Tertullian (c. A.D. 220) attributes it to Barnabas. Cyprian (c. A.D. 250), who quotes freely from all the epistles of Paul, does not quote from Hebrews at all. Augustine (c. A.D. 400), though favorably inclined toward Hebrews, writes that because it is anonymous, some "have feared to receive it into the canon of Scripture." Finally, however, Augustine's convictions as to its true worth overcame his hesitation as to its authorship, and in his treatise on Christian Doctrine (2.8.12), he clearly accepts Hebrews as Scripture. This action of Augustine settled the matter for the African churches.

3. In the Western Church, especially at Rome, Hebrews seems to have held an intermediate position: it was not regarded as written by Paul, but no other name was normally associated with it. It was assumed to be an anonymous epistle. Though Hebrews is first quoted by a member of the Western Church (Clement, c. A.D. 95), its author is never mentioned. It is even more significant that Justin Martyr (c. A.D. 150), who quotes from all of Paul's letters except Philemon, does not quote from Hebrews. In the Muratorian Canon—the earliest list of New Testament books that we possess—Paul is said to have written thirteen letters to seven churches and Hebrews is not included in the list. The greatest

scholar in the West at the end of the fourth century was Jerome, the translator of the Vulgate. He, like Augustine, after years of hesitation because of its anonymity, finally declared his faith in Hebrews as Scripture, and as to authorship, he wrote, "It makes no difference whose it is. . . ."[11]

Later Ideas of Authorship. It is clear from this brief survey that about the year A.D. 400 the Epistle to the Hebrews was firmly settled as canonical, that is, as having authority equal to the works of the apostles. Questions on the matter of authorship, however, have continued to be raised down through the centuries. Both Luther and Calvin concluded that Paul was not the author. Luther suggested Apollos, and Calvin suggested either Luke or Clement of Rome. In the years that followed, almost every writer on Hebrews has had a suggestion to make. Harnack, writing in 1900—perhaps with tongue in cheek—suggested Priscilla with the help of her husband Aquila.

The opinion held today by most scholars is that the letter is anonymous and that the most one can say is that the author "was a second-generation Christian, well-versed in the study of the Septuagint, which he interpreted according to a creative exegetical principle. He had a copious vocabulary and was master of a fine rhetorical style, completely different from Paul's."[12]

The date, though uncertain, must be before A.D. 95 or 96, since it is quoted by Clement of Rome. If Hebrews 12:4, "In your struggle against sin you have not yet resisted to the point of shedding your blood," means that no major persecution had yet taken place, we must regard the epistle as having been written before the persecution under Nero (A.D. 64), though probably not much before that date.

To Whom Was the Letter Written? Though the title "To the Hebrews" is early, it is not part of the original manuscript, but may have been inferred from the general character of the work. According to the traditional view, the readers were Hebrew Christians, possibly in the church at Rome, who, under the threat of persecution or because their first enthusiasm for Christ had waned, were tempted to relapse into Judaism. Numerous other suggestions have been made in recent years. One of the most unusual and most interesting has been made by the great French scholar Spicq who suggests that the writer had in mind particularly some group of former Jewish priests who had accepted Christ (see Acts 6:7), and who now, experiencing privation and contempt, looked back longingly to their former place of security and honor within Judaism.[13] This suggestion and others, although interesting, are based simply on hints found here and there in the epistle. It seems impossible in the present state of our knowledge to identify the readers more definitely than is done in the traditional view.

Characteristics of the Epistles: (1) Excellent literary style; (2) frequent quotations from the Greek Old Testament; (3) the tabernacle, rather than the temple, as the basic point of reference; (4) the old covenant viewed as inferior to the new, rather than (as with Paul) opposed to it; (5) special emphasis given to the priestly and mediatorial office of Christ, although the picture of Christ is rich and varied; (6) considerable stress placed on worship as the means of access to God.

Outline of the Contents of Hebrews

Part 1. The main argument (1:1–10:18)
- a. Christ is greater than angels (1:1–2:18)
- b. Christ is superior to Moses (3:1-6)
  (Digression-exhortation [3:7–4:13])
- c. Christ is our great High Priest (4:14–5:10)
  (Digression-exhortation [5:11–6:20])
- d. Christ belongs to a higher order of priesthood than Aaron— after the order of Melchizedek (7:1-28)
- e. Christ ministers in an ideal sanctuary (8:1-13)
- f. Christ offers the perfect sacrifice (9:1–10:18)

Part 2. The closing exhortation (10:19–13:25)
- a. They stand with the faithful of old (10:19–11:40)
- b. The terrors of the old covenant and the glories of the new (12:1-29)
- c. Counsel, appeal, and warning (13:1-25)

- What help is provided by the Pastoral Epistles for the organization of the modern church?

- What should be the basic qualifications of church officers today?
- How can we combat heresies such as those opposed in the Pastoral Epistles?
- How much authority should the pastor have in the local church?
- Suppose an anonymous letter of equal worth to Hebrews should be discovered today. How do you think the church should regard it?

Additional Resources

Barclay, William, *Epistle to the Hebrews.* Nashville: Abingdon Press, 1965.

Barrett, Charles F., *The Pastoral Epistles.* New York: Oxford University Press, 1963.

Bruce, Frederick F., *The Epistle to the Hebrews.* Grand Rapids, Mich.: Wm. B. Eerdmans Pub. Co., 1964.

Guthrie, Donald, *Commentary on the Pastoral Epistles.* Grand Rapids, Mich.: Wm. B. Eerdmans Pub. Co., 1957.

Harrison, Everett F., *Introduction to the New Testament.* Grand Rapids, Mich.: Wm. B. Eerdmans Pub. Co., 1964.

Kelly, J. N. D., *A Commentary on the Pastoral Epistles.* New York: Harper & Row, Publishers, Inc., 1963.

8

CHURCHES
IN TRANSITION

James, First Peter, Jude, Second Peter

The four letters to be studied in this chapter belong to a group of non-Pauline epistles that are usually called "Catholic" or "General" Epistles. The name grew out of the belief that these epistles (together with the three epistles of John) were intended for the church as a whole, rather than for particular groups or congregations. On more careful examination, however, one may well question this idea. First Peter is certainly addressed to a particular group of churches (1:1); and although particular churches are not named in the case of James, Jude, and Second Peter, it seems clear that their authors have special groups in mind.

A strong bond exists between these four epistles in that their common emphasis is on the practice, rather than on the theory of the Christian faith. Though a theological basis for the gospel is clearly assumed, this is only incidental. The chief aim of these epistles is to give counsel for day-to-day living in the dangerous and bewildering days immediately before and after the destruction of Jerusalem in A.D. 70. Then, as now, Christians needed help in facing the perplexing issues of the time.

THE EPISTLE OF JAMES

As we have seen, the early church was slow to accept certain books into that authoritative list of Scripture, which we call the canon, if there was any question as to their apostolic authorship. In addition to Hebrews (see chapter 7), the apostolic authorship of James, Jude, and Second Peter was seriously questioned during that period when the canon was being determined. It is important, therefore, to face the matter of authorship at the beginning of this study.

Which James? The epistle claims to have been written by "James, a servant of God and of the Lord Jesus Christ" (1:1). The problem of identity is raised by the fact that the New Testament speaks of three persons in the early church by the name of James: (1) James the brother of John and son of Zebedee, who was one of the Twelve (Matthew 4:21); (2) James the son of Alphaeus (Matthew 10:3), also one of the Twelve, often known as "James the Less"; (3) James the brother of our Lord, known as "the Just," who became the honored head of the church at Jerusalem (Acts 12:17; 15:13; 21:18; Galatians 1:19; 2:9, 12).

James the brother of John could hardly have been the author, since his death under Herod Antipas (c. A.D. 44) is recorded in Acts 12:1-2. Though some have placed the date of composition of James as early as A.D. 45, a date prior to A.D. 44 seems impossible. James the son of Alphaeus was considered the author by some of the early Church Fathers, but they give no reasons for their belief. Since we know almost nothing about this James, and since there is strong tradition against naming him as author, he generally is not considered a likely candidate.

From the days of Origen (died A.D. 253), the church has assumed that the author of this epistle is James the brother of Jesus. With the revival of learning after the Reformation, however, this traditional view was questioned.

Objections to the Traditional View of Authorship. The major objections are three: (1) The Greek of the Epistle of James is of a higher quality than could have been written by James, who was a Palestinian Jew. (2) There are no references in the epistle to the life, death, and resurrection of Jesus. (3) The church was slow to accept this letter into the canon.

The argument from language is weak, for we have no positive knowledge of the ability of James to use Greek. We may confidently assume that he knew Greek, since this was the common "second language" of the Mediterranean world. If the Greek of James was weak, there were many Christians in Jerusalem fully capable of translating his thoughts into the fluent Greek of the epistle.

Though it may seem strange that the brother of Jesus should write a letter in which the name of Jesus is found only twice (1:1; 2:1) and that he should fail to mention any facts of his life, death, or resurrection, this omission may be understandable for one who would not presume to use his natural relation to Jesus as a basis of authority. In spite of these omissions the teaching of the epistle frequently reminds one of the teachings of Jesus as given in the Gospels, yet James does not quote from them. The simplest explanation of this is that they are echoes of the words of Jesus that James actually heard him speak.

It is true that the church was slow in accepting this letter into the canon, but there are several explanations that seem possible: (1) The letter may have had a limited circulation in the years immediately after its composition. (2) It was largely nontheological in its subject matter. (3) With the destruction of Jerusalem and the movement eastward of the Jerusalem Christians, the prestige of James would wane, so that he could easily have remained almost unknown in the great centers of the Christian church of the second and third centuries. We conclude, therefore, that these objections are not strong enough to change the traditional view of the church, which is that we have in this letter the teaching of James, the brother of our Lord.

When Was It Written? The date of its composition depends largely upon one's view of the authorship. Though suggested dates have ranged from A.D. 45 to 120, if we assume that it was written by James the Just who was martyred in A.D. 62, it must have been written prior to that date. A date of about A.D. 60 seems likely.

The Leading Ideas in the Epistle. The message of James is intensely practical. Some have thought that James, because of his emphasis on works, was attacking Paul's teaching of salvation through faith, but in view of the nontheological character of his epistle, this seems unlikely. His emphasis is that true religion is shown by righteous action (James 1:27; 2:14-18), and in such an emphasis he was completely in accord with Paul.

Outline of Contents. The epistle is often described as a homily, or better still, as a collection of five short homilies:

1. On being tested: its values and dangers (1:2-8, 12-18)
2. On riches and poverty (1:9-11; 2:1-13; 4:8-10, 13-16; 5:1-6)
3. On believing and doing (1:19-25; 2:14-26; 3:13-18; 4:1-7,17)
4. On speech: its values and dangers (1:26-27; 3:1-12; 4:11-12; 5:12)
5. On hope, patience, and prayer (5:7-11, 13-20)

THE FIRST EPISTLE OF PETER

In contrast to its view of the Epistle of James, the early church seems never to have had any doubt about the authorship of First Peter. Second Peter 3:1 speaks of itself as the "second epistle"; it is quoted by Clement of Rome and by Polycarp, and it is listed in the canon of Eusebius as among the "accepted" books. In spite of this early and unanimous verdict of the early church, some scholars have questioned Peter's authorship on the following grounds: (1) The style and language is too good to have been written by a Galilean fisherman. (2) It is alleged that the epistle is dependent on Paul. (3) It reflects official Roman persecution which, it is said, came to that area under Trajan (c. A.D. 112). (4) References to Jesus are too few for one who had been as close to the Lord as Peter had been.

Since most of the major commentaries support the Petrine authorship, we need not repeat their arguments here, but note one important point that all of them make—namely, the participation of Silvanus. The statement of 1 Peter 5:12a is almost unanimously interpreted as meaning joint authorship, or, at the very least, that Peter had given Silvanus a rather free hand in the actual writing of the letter, even though Peter himself assumed responsibility for its contents. This Silvanus (the "Silas" of the Acts) was a trusted companion of Paul, who by the time of the composition of First Peter, was an important leader in the Christian community. It is generally assumed, then, that when Peter writes: "By Silvanus . . . I have written briefly unto you," he means that he used this great man as more than his secretary. If this assumption is correct, it answers all of the objections commonly raised against the Petrine authorship, except the matter of whether the recipients of this letter were actually suffering under an official Roman persecution.

This argument is based chiefly on 1 Peter 4:12-16, which is interpreted as meaning that Peter's readers were under persecution simply for bearing the name "Christian," as in the days of Trajan and Pliny the Younger. There is nothing in this passage, however, that requires such an assumption. The persecution mentioned seems to be unofficial, local, and largely instigated by individuals angered by the separatist actions of the Christians. Formerly, many of these Christians had entered freely into the evil life of the community; now they were separating themselves from these same evil companions, with the result that they became the object of ridicule and persecution.

The Date and Place of Writing. The traditional view is that the letter was written shortly before the Neronian persecutions (A.D. 64), but not earlier than A.D. 60. A date of A.D. 62 seems possible.

According to 1 Peter 5:13, this epistle was written from "Babylon," and the early church usually assumed that this was a cryptic allusion to Rome, as found commonly in Revelation (compare Revelation 16:19; 17:5; 18:10, 21). A few scholars[14] have argued for the Babylon in Mesopotamia, but since there is no tradition that connects Peter with Babylon, and since, on the contrary, there is early tradition for his having been in Rome, it is generally assumed that he means Rome, even though we can only surmise why he uses the term "Babylon."

The Purpose of the Letter. The purpose is concisely stated in 5:12b: ". . . exhorting and declaring that this is the true grace of God; stand fast in it." First Peter was written, therefore, to bear witness to the grace of God and to urge the followers of Christ to be strong in the face of the trials of life. The key word is "hope" (compare 1:3, 13, 21; 3:15).

Outline of First Peter. The epistle may be outlined in several ways; the following is one way of doing it:

1. Salutation (1:1-2)
2. The certainty of salvation (1:3-12)
3. The privileges of the redeemed (1:13–2:10)
4. Christian relationships (2:11–3:12)
5. Suffering and witnessing for Christ (3:13–4:19)

6. Instruction and exhortation (5:1-11)
7. Conclusion (5:12-14)

THE EPISTLE OF JUDE

Before we turn our attention to the Epistle of Jude and the Second Epistle of Peter, it is necessary to consider the relationship, if any, between them. Most scholars who have studied these two books agree that there is some sort of literary relationship between them, but there is considerable disagreement as to the nature and extent of that relationship. The most obvious literary similarity appears when Jude is compared with the second chapter of Second Peter, but other less obvious relationships become apparent when one uses the following list.

Compare Jude 2	with 2 Peter		1:2
" 3	"	"	1:5
" 5a	"	"	1:12
" 5b-19	"	"	2:1–3:3
" 24	"	"	3:14

Suggested reasons for a literary relationship are as follows: (1) Jude used Second Peter in a condensed form, in order to give his own epistle the weight of apostolic authority. (2) Peter used the Epistle of Jude, selecting pertinent passages and adding much of his own, since both writers were concerned with the same heresy. (3) Both Peter and Jude were influenced by a common oral or written pattern, by which the church sought to resist subversion of the truth.

Each of these three theories has its advocates, but, for the following reasons, the majority of scholars appear to favor the theory that Peter used portions of Jude: (1) It seems more reasonable to suppose that the longer letter (Second Peter) would use the shorter, than that Jude would omit so much of Peter's letter. (2) There are parts of Second Peter that can only be understood if one is already familiar with Jude (compare 2 Peter 2:10-11 with Jude 9). (3) There are indications that Jude was known more widely at an early date than Second Peter, which suggests that it was composed at an earlier date.

Authorship and Date. The epistle claims to have been written by Jude (or Judas), "a servant of Jesus Christ and brother of James" (1:1). Only one pair of brothers so named are known to the New Testament, and these are the brothers of Jesus (Mark 6:3). Though some scholars doubt that Jude the brother of Jesus could have written this letter (compare arguments against the authorship of James), there seems to be no valid reason for denying the traditional view.

It seems necessary to assume that the letter was composed rather late in the first century, yet early enough for Jude to have grown-up grandsons who were brought before the emperor Domitian (A.D. 81–96) on suspicion of revolutionary activities (Eusebius, *Church History,* 3.19). It seems impossible to be more precise than to suggest a date between A.D. 65 and 80.

The Purpose of the Letter. According to Jude 3 the author had planned to write a treatise on Christian doctrine but had interrupted his work to send off this hasty letter (our Epistle of Jude) to combat the activities of dangerous heretical teachers in the church. These false teachers have been variously identified as Gnostics, Cainites, Balaamites, or other unorthodox sects. The probability is that they belonged to no clearly defined sect, but were simply carnally minded persons who were guilty of both unorthodox doctrine and immoral conduct. Such persons have plagued the church through all the ages.

Jude's Use of Apocryphal Books. This is the only epistle in the New Testament that cites an apocryphal book, though we know that many such books were known and read by early Jewish and Christian communities. In verse 14 Jude refers to Enoch "in the seventh generation from Adam," and then quotes 1 Enoch 1:9 almost verbatim. In verse 9, Jude appears to be referring to another apocryphal work, the Assumption of Moses, though there is no existing text that preserves this exact passage.

An important question then is this: Does Jude regard these apocryphal works as having the same authority as Scripture? While some writers unhesitatingly affirm that he does, others disagree and point out the following: (1) Jude does not introduce his quotation in the usual manner of citing the Old Testament. He says: "It was of these also that Enoch . . . prophesied" (verse 14). Except for Matthew 15:7 (compare Mark 7:6), there is no place in the New Testament where an Old Testament quotation is introduced by the word "prophesied." Since the words "prophet" and "to prophesy" were used in a much broader sense in the first century (compare Titus 1:12, where a Cretan poet is called a "prophet"), this may mean simply that the words of Enoch have come true. (2) In Jude's reference to Enoch as the seventh from Adam, we may have no more than the repetition of an identifying phrase used twice in Enoch. (3) Even though Jude does not quote Enoch as Scripture, he appears to hold it in high esteem and is fully aware that it is highly regarded by his readers.

THE SECOND EPISTLE OF PETER

Since the relationship between Jude and Second Peter has been discussed in the preceding section, we may look immediately at the major critical question with respect to Second Peter: that of authorship.

Is this the work of Peter or of another? This is not a new question, but one that was raised as early as the third century. The literature on this one subject is so voluminous that few, even of the major commentaries, can adequately cover it. In our limited space, it is possible only to outline the principal arguments.

Evidence against Petrine authorship: (1) The style and language of Second Peter differ from that of First Peter. (2) The writer of Second Peter refers to Paul's epistles as "Scripture" at a date when, it is alleged, such a designation would not have been used. (3) The epistle borrows freely from Jude, as, it is assumed, the apostle Peter would not have done. (4) Such early Church Fathers as Origen and Eusebius expressed doubts as to its authenticity. (5) Its tone and content are deemed to be so unlike that of First Peter as to require another author.

Evidence in favor of Petrine authorship: (1) The writer identifies himself as "Simon Peter" (1:1). (2) The epistle contains several personal allusions (1:12-18), something seldom found in literature written under a fictitious name. (3) The vocabulary of Second

Peter is similar at several points to the recorded speeches of Peter in Acts. (4) In spite of differences, there also are points of similarity between First and Second Peter, both in thought and diction.

Conclusion. The slowness of the church to accept Second Peter may have been due to the isolation of the churches to which this epistle was sent, or to the restricted nature of its message, or to some other reason now unknown. Ultimately, however, the church did accept this work because it felt that in it could be heard the authentic gospel that Peter had preached. If Peter did not write it, the church was satisfied that at least he would have endorsed it and that the Spirit spoke through it.

Outline of Second Peter

1. Salutation (1:1-2)
2. The true knowledge is contained in the Christian call (1:3-21)
3. Those who trouble you are advocates of false knowledge (2:1-22)
4. In view of the coming of Christ and the Judgment, people should seek to live blamelessly and in expectation (3:1-18)

- What is the importance and relationship of apostolic authorship to inspiration?
- How do Paul and James really compare on the importance of grace and works?
- What issues of current interest are dealt with in these General Epistles?

Additional Resources

Barclay, William, *The Letters of John and Jude.* Philadelphia: The Westminster Press, 1961.
Kelly, J. N. D., *A Commentary on the Epistles of Peter and Jude.* New York: Harper & Row, Publishers, Inc., 1969.

9

LIFE, LOVE, AND LAST THINGS

The Writings of John

The writings of John quite properly are grouped together, both because they are assumed to be the work of the same author and because they probably were the last books of the New Testament to be written. Another noteworthy feature of this group of writings is that it is composed of three distinct literary forms: (1) a Gospel, (2) three epistles, and (3) an apocalypse, the only one in the New Testament. Though these three types will be considered separately, so closely are they related that when discussing one type, it frequently will be necessary to refer to the other members of the group.

THE GOSPEL OF JOHN

Theme: "I came that they may have life. . . ."

John's Gospel is perhaps the most read and the best loved of all the books of the New Testament, and, at the same time, it undoubtedly is the greatest single mystery to Bible scholars. Before we consider some of the problems, it may be helpful to outline some of the reasons why this Gospel has such universal appeal:

1. It is simple in form, limited in vocabulary, and easy to read; yet it is profound in its insight. As Luther remarked:

> John speaks as simply and straightforwardly as a child, and his words (as the wise men of the world regard them) sound very childish, but within them is a hidden majesty so great that no man, however profound his insight, can fathom or express it.[15]

2. The Fourth Gospel is more than a narrative of events and a memoir of sayings, as is the case with the Synoptic Gospels. It is a profound meditation on the meaning of the words and events in the life of Jesus as the Spirit had made them known to John and to the church. As has been said, it is "the Gospel in depth." In John's Gospel we come to see that "historical 'facts,' however well authenticated, are not themselves the life-giving Gospel; it is the interpreting Spirit, by whose activity the dead facts are made to live in believing hearts, which imparts the life of the Age to Come."[16]

3. While this Gospel omits many occurrences mentioned in the Synoptics, it nevertheless includes much that is absent from or only hinted at in the other Gospels. Among these important "inclusions" of John's Gospel are: Jesus' conversation with Nicodemus (chapter 3); Jesus' words to the woman at the well (chapter 4); Jesus' sermon on the bread of life (chapter 6); Jesus' upper room discourse (chapters 13–16); and Jesus' prayer for the church (chapter 17).

4. Although John gives us none of the parables of Jesus, he uses metaphor and symbol with consummate skill and spiritual power. Both religion and literature would be infinitely poorer without such meaningful phrases as "the light of life," "the bread of life," "living water," "the comforter," "the good shepherd," "the true vine," "the only begotten Son," and many others. While it is true that much of what John writes is, in its Semitic love of color, an echo of the Old Testament, the song that he sings is of Christ and of the new life in Christ.

5. In this Gospel special prominence is given to the deity of the Son. The Synoptics make the same claim, yet the language of the Fourth Gospel is made more emphatic by the stress that it places on *(a)* the preexistence of the Son (John 1:1, 14; 8:58; 17:5), and *(b)* its designation of the Son as the *Logos* or Incarnate Word (1:1, 14). Though John undoubtedly based his idea of the Logos on the activity of the Creative Word of Genesis, chapter one, he was fully aware that this would have added meaning for readers familiar with Greek philosophy.

The Problem of Authorship. The early church, believing as it did in the presence and power of the Holy Spirit in this Gospel, was at the same time concerned to establish its apostolic authorship, and it found the pathway to that objective strewn with difficulties. Early in the twentieth century this was considered one of the major problems of New Testament scholarship. Though its importance is not considered so great today, it still is a matter on which there is a decided difference of opinion. Quotations from two nonradical books will illustrate the continuance of the problem: A. M. Hunter, the widely read Scottish scholar, says: ". . . scarcely a reputable scholar in this country nowadays is prepared to affirm that the Fourth Gospel was written by John the Apostle."[17] However, E. E. Ellis, an able scholar in this country, writes: "John the Apostle and son of Zebedee probably was the real author of the Fourth Gospel and the three letters of John."[18] How can two such able scholars disagree so definitely?

The basis of the problem is that the author of the Fourth Gospel nowhere clearly identifies himself. The Gospel claims to have been written by "the disciple whom Jesus loved" (John 21:20, 24); the First Epistle is silent on its authorship; Second and Third John claim as their author "the Elder" (2 John, v. 1; 3 John, v. 1); Revelation states that it was written by "John" (1:1, 4, 9; 21:2). None of these passages, however, clearly states that the author was John the Apostle, son of Zebedee, though such implication is more or less strong in all cases. The arguments for and against Johannine authorship may be found in any one of the standard commentaries, and we cannot repeat them in detail here. In any consideration of these arguments it will be helpful to keep in mind the principles enunciated by Westcott as early as 1908: (1) the author was a Jew; (2) the author was a Palestinian Jew of the first century; (3) the author was an eyewitness to the events about which he writes; (4) the author was an apostle. Westcott's conclusion was that, of all the men of the New Testament known to us, John the Apostle, son of Zebedee, best fits these requirements.

About A.D. 185, Irenaeus wrote: "John the disciple of the Lord, who also reclined on his breast, . . . gave out the Gospel, living on in Ephesus of Asia." Indeed, Irenaeus ascribed all five books bearing the name of John to John the Apostle. His witness is especially significant since, as a boy in Asia Minor, he listened to the preaching of Polycarp, who himself had known the apostle John. When this and other similar traditions are considered in the light of Westcott's four principles, there seems to be no insurmountable reason for doubting the Johannine authorship. To ascribe the authorship to a shadowy figure called "John the Elder," who is completely unknown in history, requires for most people more faith than to accept the traditional view.

The Date of the Fourth Gospel. It must be obvious that the date one accepts depends largely upon one's view of the authorship. Among the radical scholars of the nineteenth century who rejected the Johannine authorship, a date as late as A.D. 170 (F. C. Bauer) seemed reasonable. Modern archaeological discoveries, however, now make such a view impossible and require a date not later than the end of the first century. The topographical details of the Gospel—with no mention of the destruction of Jerusalem—argue for an author who lived before A.D. 70, but not necessarily for the composition of the Gospel at so early a date. The date of writing therefore seems to have been in the last two decades of the first century.

The Plan of the Fourth Gospel. The central teaching of John's Gospel is that belief leads to life (3:14-16, 36; 6:47; 20:31). Since belief in a divine revelation does not come by reason but only by the testimony of those who have been the recipients of this revelation, it follows that *testimony leads to belief and belief leads to life.* This theme runs through the whole Gospel. John assumes that the testimony of the apostolic preaching and of the earlier Gospels is well known; his purpose is to show how this testimony, if accepted by faith, can lead to a new kind of life here and hereafter.

THE EPISTLES OF JOHN

Theme: "Love is of God . . . for God is Love"

There is no doubt that the Second and Third Epistles of John truly are letters, but is the First Epistle of John really a letter—even in the formal meaning of that term—or is it a sermon? Unlike the usual New Testament epistle, First John has neither an opening salutation nor a closing greeting. On the other hand, it surely is directed to a particular group and has a clearly recognizable purpose. Though it is sermonic in form, we may assume that John intended it for more than one congregation.

Authorship. With few exceptions—notably C. H. Dodd[19]—scholars are agreed that the author of the Gospel also wrote the three Epistles of John. Since we have given considerable space to a discussion of the authorship of the Gospel, these arguments need not be repeated here. We assume that John the Apostle is the author of the three epistles bearing his name.

Date of Composition. All three epistles, judged by their contents, may be dated well toward the end of the first century, perhaps A.D. 95 or 96. It has been suggested that First John may be the latest composition in the entire New Testament.

Reasons for Writing. The strong sense of urgency that pervades all three of these letters suggests that the author was forced by circumstances to write as he did. Therefore, in order to understand what he wrote, we must first ask *why* he wrote. From a study of these epistles, other books of the New Testament, and early church history, it becomes clear that near the close of the first century the Christian churches in the Roman province of Asia faced a great crisis that might have led to their ultimate destruction. The reasons for this crisis were:

1. By the year A.D. 95, most of the first-generation Christians had passed away. Many of the second-generation Christians were content to accept their faith as a satisfactory "way of life" but had never found it a consuming passion. For many of them the words of Jesus, "Most men's love will grow cold" (Matthew 24:12) had come true, and it might also be said of them: "You have abandoned the love you had at first" (Revelation 2:4).

2. There was much less desire on the part of many of the Asian Christians to be "different" (that being the New Testament meaning of "holy") from the world. A breakdown of Christian standards of ethics and morality came with this desire to be like the world.

3. Some of the churches already had been split, and those who had withdrawn had set up a rival "church," which they claimed was the true fellowship and guardian of the true doctrine. Since the spiritual requirements of this rival church were less exacting than those of Christ, it was attracting numerous adherents. Some

have called these seceders Gnostics. It is more likely that they belonged to no historic group, but were greatly attracted to religious speculation.

Principal Concepts of First John. The key word is "fellowship" (Greek, *koinonia*), which is found four times in First John (1:3, 6, 7) and only eleven times in the rest of the New Testament. In view of the current crisis in the Asian churches and its danger to true Christian fellowship, this emphasis is understandable. While it is difficult to outline this book, the general line of thought is clear: Christian fellowship, if it is to be maintained, must be built on a recognition of the true nature of God. First John emphasizes three aspects of God's nature:

1. God is Light (1:5). Since God is Light, nothing can be hidden from God. True Christian fellowship, accordingly, must be built on confession of sin (1:9-10), obedience (2:4-5), familial love (2:10), and separation from the world (2:15-17).

2. God is Life (2:25). We are God's children (3:1); as such we should resemble our Father (3:2) and live as members of God's family (3:4-24).

3. God is Love (4:8). Since God's actions toward humankind grow out of and are conditioned by love, God's children should also act in love (4:7-21), do God's commandments (5:1-3), and seek to overcome the world through faith in the Son of God (5:4-12).

The Second Epistle of John. Second John is a miniature of First John, yet there are differences. Whereas First John is addressed to a group of churches, Second John is directed to but one of them. The salutation "to the elect lady and her children" undoubtedly refers to a church (the Greek word for "church" is feminine), rather than to a person. Peter uses almost the same phrase in 1 Peter 5:13, where it is clear that he is referring to a church.

This little letter has a threefold purpose: (1) to strengthen those in the church who are "following the truth" (verses 4-6); (2) to alert them to the danger from deceivers who deny the reality of the Incarnation, and to urge them to shun such people (verses 7-11); (3) to prepare them for a visit from the Elder himself (verse 12).

The Third Epistle of John. The basic issue in Third John is not doctrine, but authority. The situation is this: A certain Diotrephes (verse 9) who was a leader, perhaps pastor, of a local congregation had rebelled against the absentee authority of the Elder, whose headquarters probably was at Ephesus. Two examples of his rebellious attitude are cited: (1) he had refused to give hospitality to a group of itinerant missionaries sent from the Elder, perhaps bearing directives; and (2) he had expelled from the church those who had received them (verse 10).

It is suggested in verse nine that John had already written a rebuking letter to Diotrephes which had been ignored. The present epistle is directed to Gaius, who seems to be the leader of the minority group. After commending Gaius for his faithful leadership, he requests that he "render any service to the brethren, especially to strangers" (verse 5). He concludes by commending Demetrius, who carried the letter.

This brief letter has significant value because it gives us a glimpse of church organization and authority, or the lack of it, toward the close of the first Christian century. It appears from this letter that the personal influence and authority of the older generation, including the Lord's surviving disciples, were breaking down and that a basis was being laid, even at that early date, for the erection of a strong, centralized hierarchical church government.

THE REVELATION OF JOHN

If we are correct in saying that the Gospel of John is the most read and best loved of all the books of the New Testament, it may likewise be said of the Revelation that it is the least read and the most misunderstood. This lack of understanding is not only true of the modern reader, but was true also of Christians of the early centuries, who hesitated long before including it in the list of authoritative Christian writings. The main reason for this difficulty lies in the fact that this book is the one New Testament representative of a special type of literature, known as *apocalyptic,* which, though familiar to first-century Jews and Christians, gradually lost favor as a literary form and ceased to be written by the end of the second century after Christ.

Characteristics of Apocalyptic Literature. The word "apocalypse" is Greek and means "unveiling," for which the Latin equivalent is "revelation." It is tragic to realize that what was written to "unveil" the eternal purposes of God in Christ soon became the most veiled book in the New Testament. The reason for this lies not in the newness of its message but in the strangeness of its form. Though the Jews produced many such books between 200 B.C. and A.D. 100, and we today possess, in whole or in part, about ten Christian apocalypses, the need for this type of writing ceased after Christianity became an accepted religion in the Roman world, and the key to understanding it was soon lost. In recent years, however, there has been most intensive study of both Jewish and Christian apocalyptic writings with the result that their basic characteristics are now clearly recognized, even though no scholar claims to have the correct interpretation of every statement. These facts are known:

1. Apocalypses were the product of days of danger and persecution. Someone has aptly called them "tracts for bad times."

2. They usually were written by an unidentified author under the name of some famous person of antiquity, such as Adam, Enoch, Moses, Baruch, or Isaiah.

3. They made much use of symbolism and highly figurative language, either as a means of "expressing the inexpressible" or as a cryptogram to disguise the contents of the writing from hostile rulers.

4. One much-used symbolic method was numerology, for in ancient times every letter of the alphabet was also a number.

5. The theology of apocalyptic literature differs from that of prophetic literature in three ways: *(a)* God is viewed as personal, but not close. *(b)* It is more concerned with the world view of humankind and events than with the local scene. *(c)* It presents a more definite view of last things than do the prophetic writings.

6. The ultimate purpose of the apocalypse is to urge patience in trouble and to build up the expectation that God will overcome evil through the heavenly Messiah.

Special Characteristics of the Revelation of John. It is now generally recognized that no correct interpretation of Revelation is possible that ignores its relationship to the larger body of apocalyptic literature. On the other hand, it is equally important to recognize the ways in which this book differs.

1. The Revelation is not pseudonymous. Its author calls himself "John," and Martin Kiddle undoubtedly is correct in saying that "nothing in the book suggests that this is a pseudonym."[20]

2. The Revelation is thoroughly Christian in theology. The author is just as much concerned for the proclamation of the gospel as was Paul, but his times are different and, therefore, he uses a different medium.

3. The Revelation is an epistle, just as truly as is Ephesians, and it is addressed to that church, along with some others. It has a salutation (1:4-8) and an epistolary conclusion (22:6-21), but while Paul wrote in straightforward prose, John writes his letter in the cryptic code-language of the apocalypse.

4. The Revelation of John stands out among other apocalyptic writings, both Jewish and Christian, as Shakespeare's *Hamlet* excels many contemporary dramas. It is a masterpiece of dramatic form, with its Prologue, Seven Acts, and Epilogue interspersed with interpretative songs of rare beauty after the fashion of the Greek drama. Compared with it, most other apocalypses are disorganized, wordy meanderings through the ancient past, or strange journeys into the dim light of the distant future.

Authorship. The discussion of this question began as far back as the times of Dionysius of Alexandria and continues to the present. It would be profitless to attempt a discussion of this problem in this brief introduction. While there are marked differences in language, style, and theological expression between the Gospel of John and the Revelation, there are also notable similarities, such as the term "Logos" for Christ (found only in John's Gospel, First John, and the Revelation). Nor may we dismiss lightly the testimony of Justin Martyr (c. A.D. 136), who attributes the Revelation to John the Apostle. If the apostle John is the author, it is entirely possible that the changes in language, style, and theology may be accounted for by the peculiar needs of the times, and by the lack of a trained secretary while he was in exile on Patmos.

Methods of Interpretation. Four major methods are recognized by scholars:

1. Preterist. This method assumes that the book has to do

exclusively with the times in which it was written, with little relevance for today.

2. Futurist. According to this view, except for chapters 1–3, the book deals exclusively with the future, the millennium, the final judgment, and the end of the world.

3. Continuous-historical. Those who follow this method believe that the Revelation presents a summary of the history of the Christian church through the ages.

4. Symbolic or Idealist. This view finds in the book the great principles of the continuous conflict between good and evil.

Each of these methods has in it some truth that should be recognized and used, but for the average reader of the Revelation it may be better to select a few guiding principles, rather than to adopt any formalized method. For this purpose, the following questions may prove helpful:

1. Would my interpretation make sense to the first-century reader?

2. Is my interpretation in accord with the general characteristics of apocalyptic literature?

3. Is my interpretation Christian in its theology?

4. Does my interpretation allow room for the Holy Spirit to speak to today's world, both about the past and also about the future?

- How does the Gospel of John speak to your need?
- Discuss the reasons given for the writing of First John. What similar problems are found in the modern church? How can this letter help solve them?
- It has been said that true human fellowship is built on true fellowship between human beings and God. Can there be fellowship, in the Christian sense, outside the church? Why? What are the characteristics of true Christian fellowship?
- It is well known that many young Christians, who know little of the Bible, are fascinated with the Revelation. Why is this dangerous? How can the church help?

Additional Resources

Barclay, William, *The Letters of John and Jude.* Philadelphia: The Westminster Press, 1961.

Barclay, William, *Letters to the Seven Churches.* Nashville: Abingdon Press, 1958.

Caird, G. B., *The Revelation of St. John the Divine,* 2nd ed., New Testament Commentaries Series. New York: Harper & Row, Publishers, Inc., 1985.

Glasson, T. F., *The Revelation of St. John.* New York: Cambridge University Press, 1965.

Ladd, G. E., *A Commentary on the Revelation of St. John.* Grand Rapids, Mich.: William B. Eerdmans Publishing Co., 1972.

Ramsay, W. M., *The Letters to the Seven Churches.* Grand Rapids, Mich.: Baker Book House, 1985.

10

COLLECTING
THE NEW TESTAMENT

Through the first nine chapters of this book we have been studying how the gospel message, first preached by a small group of Jesus' disciples, was spread through Palestine, Syria, and Asia Minor, and eventually brought to Rome. In the course of this amazing growth, numerous congregations of Christians sprang up throughout the length and breadth of the Roman world. As time passed, the first followers of Christ began to die off and the churches, wishing to preserve their direct contact with their Lord, started to collect the letters and memoirs of his closest followers. This collection eventually became the New Testament, which Christians hold to be the written deposit of the promise of Jesus (John 14:26; 16:13) in the lives and testimony of his apostles.

At this point one must ask a basic question: "How were these twenty-seven documents selected from the multitude of Christian books in circulation, and, having been selected, how were they brought together into one book?" Samuel A. Cartledge has made this comment:

> The whole question of the canon might have been greatly simplified if only God had directed the authors of the different books to put at the end of each book a little note something like this: "This book was written by John under the inspiration of the Holy Spirit, and it is meant to be Gospel number four in the New Testament." But God did not do it that way.[21]

The Christian revelation was not given on a tablet of stone, on a silken sheet let down from heaven, or on golden plates dug out of the earth, but rather it was entrusted by God, in divine wisdom, to the frail "earthen vessels" of human beings (2 Corinthians 4:7) that the power of God might be vindicated by the wonder and majesty of that which God-inspired people produced.

The purpose of this chapter is to outline the *human process*, under the guidance of the Holy Spirit, by which this collection of books was made, and to suggest in what sense this collection may be called authoritative in matters of faith and practice.

THE FIRST CENTURY

The Bible of the first-century church was the Old Testament and the Apocrypha, and it was read by most Christians in the Greek (the Septuagint version). Christian worship during this period followed closely the pattern of the Jewish synagogue. It consisted of prayer, the chanting of a psalm or hymn, readings from the Scriptures with comments or an address by the leader. Gradually this traditional pattern was changed to include the reading of apostolic letters. The reading of these writings of the apostles soon became one of the most important features of public worship, and exhortations not to neglect such reading are frequent even in the New Testament itself (1 Thessalonians 5:27; Colossians 4:16; 1 Timothy 4:13; Revelation 1:3; 2:7, 11, 17, 29; 3:6, 13, 22). Generally a local congregation would read only such apostolic communications as they themselves had received, but Colossians 4:16 indicates that churches were expected to share what they possessed with other congregations. We may suppose that copies would be made, and thus small *collections* would begin (2 Peter 3:15).

Were these apostolic writings thought of as Scripture? Since we cannot penetrate the minds of the people of the first century, we must depend on their writings for an answer. From the time of Clement of Rome (c. A.D. 95) we find early writings of the church filled with citations of New Testament writings side by side with quotations from the Old Testament. In the earliest writings there appears to be a clear distinction in the manner of introducing the Old Testament quotations and the quotations from Christian writings. In citing the former the usual method is: "The Scripture saith" or "As it stands in Scripture"; whereas Christian writers are usually cited by name or with the phrase "The Lord said." There are places, however, where a citation from the Old Testament and one from the New Testament are joined, and both are introduced as Scripture. It seems clear from these writings, therefore, that though the apostolic writings were highly treasured, they were not as yet regarded as Scripture in the same sense as the Old Testament. A well-known quotation of Papias will serve to illustrate this attitude. Writing about A.D. 120, he said: "I did not think that I could profit so much from the contents of books as from the utterances of a living and abiding voice."

Though most Christians likely preferred the "living and abiding voice" of an apostle, nevertheless collections of Christian writings began to be made even during their lifetime. Before the end of the first century two collections certainly were in circulation: (1) a collection of certain of the epistles of Paul, and (2) a collection of the Gospels. Which came first is still a matter of debate.

THE SECOND CENTURY

Important for a study of the canon are the following second-century works: The Epistle of Barnabas, The Epistle of Ignatius and Polycarp, The Didache (Teaching) of the Twelve Apostles, The Shepherd of Hermas, The Martyrdom of Polycarp, The Epistle to Diognetus, fragments from the lost writings of Papias as given by Eusebius, and The Gospel of Truth.

From these books we have an idea of the increasing use being made of the New Testament writings in the first half of the second century. Though as yet there was no authoritative collection of writings accepted by all the churches, the idea of a collection was certainly present, and influences were in operation in the early church that eventually led to a strong feeling of need for such a collection.

Why Did the Church Feel the Need of a Canon? Before answering this, we must examine more closely the meaning of the term "canon." The word is derived from the Greek *kanon,* which in its simplest meaning refers to a "reed" or "cane" such as grew in the marshes of the Mediterranean world. Reeds with markings on them became the basic measuring tools of the ancient world, and this idea of a measuring tool soon was transferred to the things thus measured in the metaphorical sense with a list of measured or authoritative rules of faith (Galatians 6:16) or writings. After a study of eight common meanings of the word "canon," Souter believes that the usual church meaning was "a list of biblical books which may be read in public services at a church, and, if such be produced with the authority of a synod or council, of the church."[22]

The following factors leading to the development of such a list were present in the life of the early church:

1. The Old Testament served as a model, for it was a group of books already accepted as the authoritative word of God, both by Jews and Christians.

2. To the Christian church the words of Christ, through the apostles, held a place of authority equal with the Old Testament. Hence the words of the apostles were invested with the authority of Christ. Furthermore, at an early age, the church enlarged the apostolic circle to include, in addition to the Twelve, other apostolic men such as Luke, Mark, Paul, James, and Jude.

3. Since these apostolic writings were widely used both in church worship and teaching, the need for a commonly accepted list was evident to many.

4. The need for defense against hostile opponents from without and erroneous opinions from within made it imperative that the church, in order to strengthen its position, establish a list of acceptable Christian writings.

The Influence of Marcion. One of the most able of the false teachers of that day was a Christian leader from Pontus named Marcion. He arrived in Rome about A.D. 140, and soon had gathered about him a substantial following of disciples committed to the Gnostic type of Christianity. Marcion was strongly influenced by the Gnostic idea of dualism, which assumed the existence of two gods, one responsible for the material creation with all of its evil, the other being pure spirit and far removed from the world of matter. Marcion identified the former deity with the Jehovah of the Old Testament and the latter with the God and Father of our Lord. In rejecting the God of the Old Testament, Marcion also rejected the Old Testament itself. In addition, he began a systematic eradication of all traces of Old Testament influence from current Christian writings in the belief that these might infect his followers. The result of his efforts was his canon, the approved list of books that he recommended to his disciples. This list contained only one Gospel (an expurgated edition of Luke) and ten epistles of Paul, excluding the Pastorals. All the other New Testament books Marcion judged to be tainted with the Jewish doctrine of Jehovah worship, and hence were unchristian.

Marcion, after a time, was convicted of heresy, and his doctrines were condemned by the church. But, for our investigation, the reaction of Christian leaders to his canon of Scripture was most important. It probably is incorrect to say, as some have done, that Christian leaders at Rome produced their canon in opposition to that of Marcion; but it is true that Marcion's heretical canon provided a needed incentive to state the orthodox position with regard to an authoritative list of Christian writings.

In 1740, L. A. Muratori published a manuscript that he found in the Ambrosian Library at Milan. F. F. Bruce has described this manuscript as "an orthodox counterblast to Marcion."[23] This document—known as the Muratorian fragment—is mutilated at the beginning, but it contains a list of New Testament books. The list apparently began with Matthew and Mark, since it mentions Luke as the "third" Gospel; it continues by listing John, the Acts, thirteen letters of Paul, Jude, First and Second John, the Revelation of John, and the Revelation of Peter. The date of this fragment is believed to be between A.D. 170 and 200. If so, we find that at that date, in Rome, only five books of our New Testament (Hebrews, James, First and Second Peter, and Third John) were not yet included in the list of Christian writings commonly used in the churches. This does not mean that the Roman church had judged these missing books to be uninspired or without authority. It is more probable that as yet they were not well known.

THE CLOSING OF THE CANON:
A.D. 200–400

The church, as it existed in the third and fourth centuries, may be viewed as divided into three major areas: the Eastern, with its headquarters at Syrian Antioch, the Southern, with Alexandria in Egypt as its center, and the Western, with its seat of authority at Rome. In each area there were influences on the churches that eventually led them to establish an approved list of New Testament books. The procedure, however, was different in each of the three areas.

1. The Eastern or Syrian church began with a list somewhat smaller than that which it ultimately adopted. At first, this list included only eighteen books as follows: four Gospels, the Acts, and thirteen epistles of Paul. Later, as church usage made it necessary, four more were added: Hebrews, James, First Peter, and First John. Last of all were added Second Peter, Jude, Second and Third John, and Revelation. There was never any formal closing of the canon in the Eastern churches.

2. The Southern or North African church followed an opposite course. It began with a list of more than twenty-seven books and gradually reduced this to the list that we have today. The earliest list of Christian writings included First Clement, Epistle of Barnabas, Revelation of Peter, Shepherd of Hermas, Acts of Paul, and Teaching of the Twelve Apostles. Certain writings ceased to be widely used in the churches, and the Easter Letter of Athanasius, Bishop of Alexandria, in A.D. 367 identified the twenty-seven books of our present New Testament as alone being canonical.

3. The Western or Roman church followed a middle-of-the-road course. For many years the major problem was the question of the inclusion of Hebrews. When, under the influence of Augustine, this epistle was accepted as written by Paul or under Paul's influence, the matter was settled. With the inclusion of Hebrews, the Roman canon came to be identical with our twenty-seven books.

This common agreement upon the canon, arrived at by different paths and on the level of the local churches, was ratified at a series of councils: Laodicea (367), Hippo (393), Carthage (397), and again at Carthage in 419. It is important to emphasize again that these councils did not decide what books were to be included in the New Testament; they simply ratified what the churches had already decided as they recognized the voice of the Spirit in certain writings and missed it in others.

The Principles of Selection. We have said that this matter was decided on the level of the local churches. We must now examine the principles that guided the churches in making this selection. Though the basic test of whether or not a certain writing should be accepted as authoritative is inspiration, it is easy to understand that this is not a test that fallible human beings can easily apply. Inspiration was not in itself considered as a test, but rather the spiritual environment in which human tests were applied. To put the matter another way, the early church believed that as it applied tests to Christian writings it did so under the influence of the ever-present Spirit and in response to the teachings of Jesus (Matthew 16:18-19; John 16:13). The following tests, applied consciously or unconsciously, were the human means employed by the churches.

1. *Apostolicity.* Apparently the first question asked of any writing was this: "Was it written by an apostle or by one in close relation to the apostles?" Since Jesus himself had appointed the Twelve, any authentic memoir by this group would give the church direct communication with the acts and words of Jesus. A recognition of the importance of this principle helps to understand the great concern of the early church over questions of apostolic authorship.

2. *Usage.* Since the major purpose of a canon was to provide the churches with acceptable and authoritative Christian documents to be used in public worship, it was important that every work on the approved list have permanent value for public reading, as well as for private devotions and study. The application of this test may well have excluded from the canon some of the writings even of the apostles. We know, for example, that Paul wrote more letters to churches than are included in our New Testament (see chapter 4), but some of these, though regarded as inspired, may have been judged by the churches as too personal, too local in teaching, or for some other reason not useful for public reading.

3. *Conformity to Christian Doctrine and Morality.* Since the church preached a gospel and followed a pattern of Christian life for many years before there were Christian writings, a writing was judged to be worthy of inclusion in the approved list if it conformed to these accepted standards. The application of this test

eventually excluded such widely read—and somewhat worthy—writings as The Shepherd of Hermas, The Epistle of Barnabas, The Teaching of the Twelve Apostles, and The Apocalypse of Peter.

The Meaning and Value of the Canon for Today. The canon is that list of Christian writings that the church, under the guidance of the Holy Spirit, came to recognize as most fully and most effectively incorporating the supreme revelation of God in Jesus Christ.

The twenty-seven books of the New Testament canon do not contain the *total* revelation of God in Christ, for, as the Fourth Gospel states (John 21:25), it would take a library as big as the world to contain the whole story. Nevertheless, nothing is missing from these twenty-seven books that is needed for humankind's salvation.

Furthermore the canon consists of twenty-seven divine/human documents. The early church recognized this fact, but it is not always admitted today. Bernard Ramm puts the matter succinctly:

> No theologian has ever lived who can tell the church how to draw any sort of line in Scripture between the human and the divine. The church is shut up to confess that at the same time the graphe is the word of God and the word of man and must avoid all attempts to explicate the mystery of this union.[24]

Again, it cannot be said that inclusion in the canon gives a book authority. The very opposite is true. Because a writing was believed to be authoritative, it was included in the canon. Authority always precedes canonicity. After giving full recognition to all of the foregoing statements, it may be confidently said that the canon has significant value for women and men today.

1. It contains virtually all that has survived of the first-century record of the life and ministry of Christ and of the teaching of the early church.

2. No other Christian writings have ever offered these twenty-seven books serious competition as witnesses to the living Word.

3. The New Testament canon uniquely preserves for all generations the essential truths proclaimed by the apostles as to the way by which men and women may be saved.

4. It was the belief of the early church that when these words

were read and interpreted by the Holy Spirit, God spoke through them. To this the ages have replied: "Amen!"

- What was the reason for the concern of the early church about apostolic authorship?
- Why should the canon of Scripture be closed when the Holy Spirit is still leading inspired disciples to write the story of Christ's church and to give valuable counsel on church problems and doctrine?
- How did the principle of usage function in the development of the canon? If the average Christian followed this principle today, what more recent books might be included in the canon? What books could be eliminated? Why?
- What present Christian needs are unmet by the Scriptures?
- After reading portions from First Clement, Epistle of Barnabas, or Shepherd of Hermas, seek to discover their positive value and also why they were excluded from the canon.
- Is the canon more or less important to the modern church than it was to the early church?

Additional Resources

Bruce, Frederick F., *The Books and the Parchments.* Westwood, N.J.: Fleming H. Revell Co., 1950.

Harrison, Everett F., *Introduction to the New Testament.* Grand Rapids, Mich.: Wm. B. Eerdmans Pub. Co., 1964.

James, Montague, R., *The Apocryphal New Testament.* New York: Oxford University Press, 1924.

11

THE TRANSMISSION AND RESTORATION OF THE WRITINGS

In the preceding chapters frequent mention has been made of the "books" of the New Testament, but originally these were not printed books; they were *manuscripts* (handwritten). It was almost exactly fourteen centuries from the time Paul wrote his letter to the Romans (A.D. 56) to the publication of this or any portion of the Bible printed from movable type (A.D. 1456). Until that time all copies of the Bible were handwritten. In spite of care, mistakes were made by the scribes; these mistakes were recopied with new mistakes added until there were many variations in the existing manuscripts. How then can we be confident that we now possess a true copy of what the author originally wrote? One might answer that this has been guaranteed by the overall supervision of the Holy Spirit. Just as God chose to deliver the divine revelation through the hearts and minds of human beings, so God has chosen to guard this revelation and transmit it to future generations by devoted believers.

We see the hand of the Spirit in three ways: (1) The scribes who did the copying, in spite of their fallibility, were for the most part deeply religious and, conscious of their godly task, exercised unusual care in their work. (2) More manuscripts of the New Testament have been preserved for us than of any other book or collection of books of that age. (3) The science of textual criticism has now developed to a point where highly skilled specialists, when confronted with many variants, are able to determine with remarkable precision the correct reading.

THE TRANSMISSION OF THE TEXT

No original copy (autograph) of any book of the New Testament is known to exist at the present time, and, since most originals were written on highly perishable papyrus, it is hardly likely that any will be found in the future. Since we must depend on copies made from copies, it is important to consider first the materials and methods employed in this process.

Materials Used by the Scribes. (1) *Papyrus.* Until the fourth century A.D., papyrus was the common writing material of the Mediterranean world. It was produced from a tall reed that grew in swampy areas, especially in the delta of the Nile. It was used in single sheets or in rolls (scrolls) of about twenty sheets pasted together. Papyrus was cheap and therefore was widely used; it was also fragile, with the result that little of it has survived except in the extremely dry climate of Egypt. (2) *Vellum.* From the fourth to the fourteenth century most manuscripts were written on vellum (parchment), though papyrus continued to be used in private correspondence and in business. Vellum properly means calfskin, but the general term came to be used for any writing material made from the skin of an animal. (3) *Paper.* Apparently the Chinese were the first to produce the writing material made from hemp or flax that we call paper. Introduced into Europe in the twelfth century, it largely displaced vellum by the fifteenth century.

Manuscript Materials Available for Study. The nearly five thousand manuscripts now known to exist are usually divided into three major groups: (1) Greek Manuscripts (MSS); (2) versions, that is, translations into languages other than Greek; (3) quotations from the group commonly referred to as the Church Fathers.

1. Greek Manuscripts. The oldest-known Greek manuscript is a very small fragment containing five verses from John's Gospel (18:31-33, 37-38). It is known as the John Rylands Papyrus. It is dated about A.D. 150, and its chief value is that it "proves the existence and use of the Fourth Gospel during the first half of the second century in a provincial town along the Nile, far removed from its traditional place of composition (Ephesus in Asia Minor)."[25]

Other important Greek papyrus manuscripts of the second and third centuries are The Chester Beatty Biblical Papyri. These were discovered in 1930–31, and contain portions of the Gospels, nine Epistles of Paul, and Revelation. One of the most exciting finds in recent years was the Bodmer Papyri, discovered in 1955–56, which contains portions of John's Gospel, Jude, First and Second Peter, Acts, James, and the three Epistles of John. These manuscripts are dated by their editors as being from A.D. 175 to 225.

From the fourth and fifth centuries, when vellum was more commonly used, a greater abundance of manuscript material has survived. Most of these are in book form (codex), rather than scrolls, and they are called *uncials* because they employ a rather formal method of writing entirely in capital letters. A few of the more important uncial codices are listed below.

Sinaiticus (Codex Aleph) was discovered by Tischendorf in 1859 in the monastery of St. Catherine on Mt. Sinai. At one time it contained the entire Bible, but many leaves had been burned as waste paper before Tischendorf rescued it. In this way, parts of the Old Testament were destroyed, but the entire New Testament has survived. This manuscript, believed to have been written in the fourth century, was sold by the Soviet government in 1933 to the British Museum for more than $500,000.

Alexandrinus (Codex A) is a manuscript of the fifth century, also in the British Museum. It contains both Testaments and is almost complete.

Vaticanus (Codex B). This manuscript, which was produced about the same time as Sinaiticus, has been in the Vatican Library at Rome for at least 500 years. It is considered by many scholars to be our most valuable single manuscript, even though it lacks the New Testament from Hebrews 9:14 onward.

Ephraemi (Codex C). This fifth century manuscript is often called *Ephraemi Rescriptus* (that is, "rewritten"). It is one in which the original biblical text was erased sometime during the twelfth century, and in its place were written thirty-eight treatises of St. Ephraem, a Syrian church authority of the fourth century. By the use of chemicals, ultraviolet light, and much patient labor, scholars have been able to decipher this valuable biblical text. As one scholar wryly remarked, "This was not the first time nor the last that a sermon has obscured the Bible."

Bezae (Codex D). This manuscript of the fifth century is named after its former owner, Theodore Beza, the successor to Calvin as the leader of the Genevan church. It contains many unusual readings believed to have been commonly found in texts of the Western church. It contains most of the Gospels and Acts, with a small fragment of Third John.

The Freer Manuscript (Codex W). This, the only major codex in the United States, is in the Freer Museum of the Smithsonian Institution in Washington, D.C. It contains the Gospels and is believed to date from the late fourth or early fifth century.

2. Versions. Translations of the Greek manuscripts were made at a very early date, especially by missionaries as an aid to evangelization. Since some of these versions were made as early as the second or third centuries, they were based on manuscripts older than any we now possess; hence they often are a valuable help in checking Greek manuscripts.

The two earliest and most important versions are the Syriac and the Latin. Syriac, a Semitic language much like Hebrew and Aramaic, was the language spoken in the Eastern branch of the Christian church. Translations into Syriac dialects were made as early as the middle of the second century.

Latin was the language of the Western church, and the Greek New Testament was translated into this tongue before the end of the second century. The most important of these Latin versions is the notable revision of Old Latin texts made by Jerome, which is known as the Vulgate edition. It was produced in A.D. 382 at the request of Pope Damasus. More than eight thousand manuscripts of the Vulgate are now known to scholars.

Other early versions were produced in Coptic (Egyptian), Gothic (Germanic), Armenian, Georgian, Ethiopic, Slavonic, Arabic, and Anglo-Saxon.

3. Quotations from the Church Fathers. In their commentaries, sermons, debates with opponents, and treatises, this group of church authorities used many quotations from Scripture texts that they possessed. B. M. Metzger, a prominent biblical scholar, has observed:

So extensive are these citations that if all other sources for our knowledge of the text of the New Testament were destroyed, they would be sufficient alone for the reconstruction of practically the entire New Testament.[26]

Since these leaders quoted from texts used in their own locality, their citations are of great value in determining when and where various types of texts were used. Since they often quoted from memory, however, their citations must be used with caution.

THE CORRUPTION OF THE TEXT

In spite of the care, skill, and religious devotion that most of the scribes used in the task of copying the sacred text, they were subject to influences that often led to errors in their work. Most of their errors were trivial, but the cumulative effect of them, when recopied many times and with new errors added, resulted in a text often seriously corrupted. Most of these scribal errors were unintentional, but some of them resulted from deliberate changes in cases where the scribe assumed that he was restoring the original reading.

1. Unintentional Corruptions. For convenience, most of these may be classified as errors of the eye, the ear, and understanding.

Errors of the Eye: The earliest of the manuscripts were written entirely in capital letters (called "uncials"). This, perhaps, was in imitation of inscriptions in stone. Unfortunately, in order to conserve space, there were neither marks of punctuation nor spaces between words. Even though the scribes were used to this method, it was not uncommon for the eye to betray them into making the division between words at the wrong places, especially if the resultant reading made sense.

Errors of the Ear: It was common practice for the books to be reproduced by dictation. This often led to confusion of two words that sounded alike but were spelled differently and had different meanings, such as the English words "their" and "there," or "red" and "read," or "great" and "grate." See Revelation 1:5, where the King James Version has "washed us from our sins" and revised versions have "loosed us from our sins." The Greek words for "wash" and "loose," though spelled differently, sound alike, and both readings make sense.

Errors of Understanding and Judgment: This class includes unintentional transposition of words, substitution of synonyms, changes in sequence of words, and marginal notes mistakenly incorporated into the text (compare John 5:4 and the note in the Revised Standard Version).

2. Intentional Changes. B. M. Metzger, in the book already cited, comments, "Odd though it may seem, scribes who thought were more dangerous than those who wished merely to be faithful in copying what lay before them."[27] Indeed, many of the most serious corruptions of the text have resulted from the work of copyists who assumed that, in altering the text, they were correcting an error of an earlier scribe. Among the more common intentional changes are "corrections" of spelling and grammar, aimed at harmonizing an Old Testament quotation with the Greek Septuagint, at harmonizing a statement of Jesus in one Gospel with that given in another, or at "clearing up" historical or geographical difficulties. A classic example of the last-named type of alteration is the change made by Origen (*Commentary on John,* 1:28) where his text reads "Bethany beyond Jordan," but since he knew of no such place, he assumed that the proper reading should be "Bethabara." Long after Origen's day, archaeologists discovered the ruins of a Bethany east of Jordan and proved Origen guilty of an error even though his intentions were good. Not all intentional changes, however, were made in such good faith. Mention has already been made (see chapter 10) of the changes made by Marcion in support of his Gnostic views. The text of the seventh chapter of First Corinthians is one of the most corrupt, apparently because neither those who approved of asceticism nor those who disapproved of it were satisfied with Paul's views. To what extent alterations were made in the interest of peculiar doctrinal views is difficult to say. Some scholars feel that this was common practice; others are equally certain that such practice was rare.

THE RESTORATION OF THE TEXT

As early as the fourth century the Latin manuscripts were so filled with variant readings that Pope Damasus commissioned the scholar Jerome to revise them and produce a Latin version that would be true to the original Greek. The Latin Vulgate ("common") Edition that resulted was the standard Bible of the church in the West until the sixteenth century. With the advent of printing, the renewed interest in the Greek classics, and the Protestant Reformation came the desire to produce a printed *Greek* New Testament. But, among the many manuscripts of the New Testament available, there was no one that was generally accepted as standard by all branches of the church. Faced with this problem, a few devout and courageous scholars began the difficult task of clearing existing texts of corruptions in order that the text of Scripture might be restored to its original form. From such simple beginnings the scientific study of the text of Scripture developed into what is now known as "textual criticism." The textual critic is concerned solely with the problem of discovering what the author of each New Testament book wrote and is not concerned with the interpretation of the author's meaning. It is easy to see that such study of the Scripture text is fundamental to all other study, for we must first be certain that we have the exact words of Scripture before we seek to interpret their meaning.

The Scientific Study of the Text. Early printed Greek Testaments were made from a few late manuscripts, and by the eighteenth century serious attempts were made to produce a revised text based on many newly discovered manuscripts. The work progressed slowly, and, in spite of severe opposition, the basic principles of textual criticism were developed. Between 1841 and 1872 one scholar alone (Tischendorf) published eight editions of the Greek New Testament, twenty-two volumes of texts of biblical manuscripts, and more than 150 books and articles relating to biblical criticism! For those interested further in textual criticism, an excellent primer is now available in J. H. Greenlee's book which is listed in the bibliography.

SOME RESULTS
OF TEXTUAL CRITICISM

1. The "received text" *(Textus Receptus),* which was the basis of the King James Version, has been shown to be a good text, but not the best text. F. J. A. Hort, in the introduction to the Westcott and Hort edition of the Greek New Testament, concludes by saying:

> The proportion of words virtually accepted on all hands as raised above doubt is very great; not less, on rough computation, than seven-eighths of the whole. The remaining eighth, therefore, formed in great part by changes of order and other comparative trivialities, constitutes the whole area of criticism."[28]

2. Nevertheless, since we are concerned with the word of God, the church can never be satisfied with even a fraction of the text in doubt. Textual criticism has reduced uncertainty in this residue to a point where, to quote Mr. Hort again, it can be said that: "Substantial variation can hardly form more than a thousandth part of the entire text."[29]

3. New biblical material is being discovered and new techniques for study are being devised, so that one may reasonably expect a continual reduction in the proportion of the text still subject to uncertainty.

4. As the study of the text continues, there will be constant need for revised versions in modern languages.

5. Textual criticism has proved beyond a shadow of a doubt that we have, in all important essentials, the New Testament text as it was originally written. No significant doctrine or historical fact in the New Testament has been changed by this study, but, on the contrary, the basis of our trust in the Scripture has been undergirded and our faith strengthened thereby.

• What writing materials did the early scribes use, and how did these affect the number and type of manuscripts that we now possess?

• How would you answer someone's criticism that the Bible was full of errors and contradictory statements?

- What are the values and dangers in the use of quotations from the early Church Fathers?
- What effect did the errors of the early scribes have upon the biblical text? How serious are errors of interpretation made by Christians today as they preach and teach?
- Why is it necessary for new versions of the English Bible to be made from time to time?

Additional Resources

Bruce, Frederick F., *Are the New Testament Documents Reliable?* Grand Rapids, Mich.: Wm. B. Eerdmans Pub. Co., 1954.

Greenlee, J. Harold, *Introduction to New Testament Textual Criticism.* Grand Rapids, Mich.: Wm. B. Eerdmans Pub. Co., 1964.

Metzger, Bruce M., *The Text of the New Testament: Its Transmission, Corruption, and Restoration.* New York: Oxford University Press, 1964.

12

THE ENGLISH
NEW TESTAMENT

The introduction of Christianity into Britain is attributed traditionally either to Paul, Peter, Simon Zelotes, or Joseph of Arimathea. But it is more probable that the faith was brought to Britain first by Roman legionaries and merchants. Progress appears to have been slow until the arrival of Augustine (A.D. 597), when new impetus was given to the struggling Christian communities.

The Bible of these early missionaries was, of course, the Latin Vulgate. Translation from Latin was hindered, first, by the fact that there was no English language in the true meaning of the term, and, second, by the fact that few could read even their own native tongue. There were, however, attempts to tell the stories of the Bible through the songs of men like Caedmon (c. A.D. 670) and a translation of the Gospel of John into Anglo-Saxon by Bede.

King Alfred the Great (A.D. 871–901), an unusually able and literate ruler, published a code of laws that were introduced by an English version of the Ten Commandments, followed by translations of other passages from both Testaments.

The Anglo-Saxon language used in that day as English seems almost completely alien to us now, but the Norman Conquest brought a linguistic revolution that changed it into a form that is intelligible today. Compare a few verses of Matthew 13:3-4 in Anglo-Saxon with the opening words of the Lord's Prayer as written after the Conquest:

Sothlice ut eode sawere his saed to sawenne. And tha he seow, sumu hie feollon with weg, and fuglas comon and aeton tha. (From the Wessex Gospels)

Oure Fader that are in heuene, halewed be thi name. Thi kyngdom come to us. Thi wylle be don, as in heuene, and in erthe. (From a fourteenth-century translation)

The first translation of the whole Bible into English is associated with the name of John Wycliffe (also written Wyclif and Wiclif). Wycliffe, who was born about 1330 and who died in 1384, is regarded as the greatest Oxford theologian of his time. His translation was in manuscript form and was made directly from the Latin. Though this handwritten version was soon superseded by other versions in printed form, his was the first attempt to put the entire Bible into the vernacular. Wycliffe's views were soon condemned by the church as heretical and the reading of his version was banned. Sometime after his death, the Council of Constance (1415) ordered that his writings be burned. His body was later disinterred and burned, and the ashes were cast into the river Swift. But the "morning star of the Reformation" had risen, and soon the dark clouds of biblical illiteracy would be scattered.

ANCESTORS OF
THE KING JAMES VERSION

The Tyndale Version. Perhaps the most important name in the long list of those who have contributed to the translation of the English Bible is that of William Tyndale (c. 1490–1536). At Oxford he studied under Erasmus, who in 1516 published the first printed Greek New Testament. Even in his early youth Tyndale had felt the need for an English version of the Scriptures, and his studies under Erasmus turned this interest into a burning passion. All his attempts to make such a translation, however, were met by the unyielding opposition of the clergy. It was during a dispute with one of the clergy that he uttered his prophetic words: "If God spare my life, ere many years I will cause a boy that driveth the plough shall know more of the Scripture than thou dost."

Since it proved impossible for Tyndale to carry out his work in England, he moved his residence to the Continent. There, beginning at Wittenberg, later at Hamburg, and finally at Cologne he finished his translation of the New Testament, which was published at Worms in 1526. In October of that year, many of the first copies were burned by order of the Bishop of London.

The edition of 1534 is of particular importance since its English style left an indelible mark on all subsequent English versions. It has been said that "nine-tenths of the Authorized New Testament is still Tindale [Tyndale], and the best is still his."[31]

Opposition to Tyndale, however, was increasing, and on May 21, 1535, he was kidnapped from the safety of the free city of Antwerp and imprisoned in the fortress of Vilverde near Brussels. Here he languished until October 6, 1536, when, in the trenchant words of John Foxe, "he was brought forth to the place of execution, was there tied to the stake, and then strangled first by the hangman, and afterwards with fire consumed . . . crying thus at the stake with a fervent zeal and a loud voice: 'Lord, open the King of England's eyes.' "

The Coverdale Version. During the eighty-five years between the appearance of Tyndale's version and the publication in 1611 of the King James Version, several notable English versions appeared. The first of these was prepared by Miles Coverdale (1488–1569). Next to Tyndale, the English Bible owes its greatest debt to Coverdale. He had the honor of publishing (1535) the first printed edition of the whole Bible in English. Because his nature was less passionate and more conciliatory, he was able not only to survive both Catholic and Protestant persecutions but also to find acceptance for his edition. It is ironic that a year before Tyndale was executed, Coverdale's Bible, which depended much on Tyndale's version, was allowed to circulate freely in England.

"Matthew's" Bible (1537). This was a composite work produced by John Rogers, a friend of Tyndale. In order to hide his indebtedness to Tyndale's forbidden version, he used the pen-name of Thomas Matthew. This version may well be called the first "authorized" edition since, through the influence of Archbishop Cramner and Thomas Cromwell, it was published under royal license.

The Great Bible (1539). Miles Coverdale was editor-in-chief of this project, which was largely a revision of "Matthew's" Bible minus certain controversial notes. It measured 16½ by 11 inches and, according to Cromwell's command, was to be made available "in some convenient place . . . whereas your parishioners may most commodiously resort to the same."

The Geneva Bible (1560). During the latter part of the reign of Henry VIII a reaction set in, and a royal decree of 1546 forbade ownership of either Tyndale's or Coverdale's version. Though there was a brief easing of restrictions under Henry's successor (Edward VI), he was followed on the throne by Mary, a Catholic, during whose bloody reign (1552–1558) the reading of the English Bible was strictly forbidden.

During this troublesome period Geneva became the gathering place for many church leaders and scholars with strong Protestant views. Here John Calvin was at the height of his influence, and renowned scholars such as Theodore Beza worked. Among those who fled to the safety of Geneva was William Whittingham, brother-in-law of Calvin and later minister to the English congregation in Geneva. Largely through his influence a small and inexpensive English version was published, subsequently called the Geneva Bible. It was so popular that it went through at least 140 editions. This was the Bible known to Shakespeare and John Bunyan, the one brought to America by the Puritan pilgrims. It is often called the "Breeches Bible" because it reads in Genesis 3:7: "Adam and Eve sewed figge tree leaves together and made themselves breeches."

The Bishops' Bible (1568). Because of its strong Protestant bias, the Geneva Bible was unacceptable to the leaders of the English church. Accordingly, under the leadership of the Archbishop of Canterbury, a version was produced by a committee of bishops and made available to the churches in 1568. Though a number of excellent scholars were engaged in the work, the resultant version was of unequal value; it was pedestrian in spirit and never a serious challenge to the Genevan version.

THE KING JAMES VERSION (1611)

For many English-speaking Christians the King James or Authorized Version is *the* Bible. They regard most other translations with disfavor and often with suspicion. This high opinion cannot be explained solely on the grounds of familiarity, for many who are quite familiar with other versions and readily admit their superior accuracy still find in this older version the sound and spirit of the biblical faith. These qualities of language and spirit were not achieved by some miraculous powers given to the translators in 1611, but were latent in the bud that Wycliffe first nurtured, that Tyndale and Coverdale watered, and that at last, under the bright sun of the Elizabethan age, burst into glorious bloom. If ever there was a "fullness of time" for the appearance of a superb translation of the English Bible, it was during the reign of James I of England (James VI of Scotland), successor to Elizabeth, for "Men who heard and loved the rich cadences of Shakespeare's lines could scarcely have produced a crabbed literal rendering of the Bible."[32]

Acting on the suggestion of Dr. John Reynolds, King James I, a Puritan, gave royal approval for a new translation of the Bible with the hope that it might bring harmony between the Anglican and Puritan factions that troubled his reign. The actual work began in 1604 with the appointment of fifty-four scholars who were divided into six companies. To each company was assigned a section of the Bible, including the Apocrypha. Eventually the whole was placed in the hands of Dr. Thomas Bilson, Bishop of Winchester, and Dr. Myles Smith, Bishop of Gloucester, who completed the final work of editing the translation which was sent to press in 1611.

In order to evaluate the King James Version, several important points must be kept in mind: (1) The preface clearly states that it was not intended to be a new translation, but a revision of the Bishops' Bible. (2) The language, since it was dependent on older versions, was in some respects archaic, even in 1611. (3) When it appeared, it met opposition and criticism as had all other versions. The violence of this opposition may be seen in the words of Dr. Hugh Broughton, a noted Hebrew scholar, who said, "It is so ill done. Tell his Majesty that I had rather be rent in pieces with wild horses, than any such translation by my consent should be urged upon poor churches." (4) Eventually it won its way into the hearts of English-speaking Protestants on sheer merit and reigned supreme for nearly three centuries.

Since the King James Version, by its own admission, was a

revision and not a translation, it was inevitable that a new translation would be desired. It was common knowledge among scholars that this version was based on an inferior Greek text largely drawn from relatively late manuscripts. Except for the Vatican manuscript, to which Erasmus referred only once, none of the major Greek manuscripts were used and most of them were not even known to scholars in 1611. During the eighteenth and nineteenth centuries great advances were made in the discovery and study of ancient manuscripts, and numerous Greek texts were published based on such textual work. The time was ripe for a new version.

In 1870, following a motion made by Dr. Wilberforce, Bishop of Winchester, a committee was formed to lay plans for a new version. American as well as British scholars were invited to participate in the undertaking. The Revised Version of the New Testament was published in 1881 and of the Old Testament four years later.

The Revised Version represented a great advance over the King James Version in the accuracy of its translation, but its English style was often pedantic and stiff. As a result, acceptance of it, and of its American counterpart (The American Standard Version of 1901), was slow. Neither of these revisions ever replaced the King James Version in popular esteem.

TWENTIETH-CENTURY VERSIONS

Space permits the mention of only a few of these, even though several were of high quality and were widely used.

The Twentieth-Century New Testament (1902). This, the first of a series of "modern English" versions, was a good translation, even though the translators, for the most part, were not notable Greek scholars.

The New Testament in Modern Speech (1903). This was a private translation by Dr. Richard Weymouth, fellow of University College, London, which did not seek to supplant either the King James or the Revised versions. Weymouth referred to it as "a succinct and compressed running commentary (not doctrinal) to be used side by side with its older compeers."

The New Testament: A New Translation (1913) by the brilliant

Scottish scholar James Moffatt. The Old Testament appeared in 1924. It is characterized by freedom and vigor and, on occasion, by Scottish idiom. It has been much criticized by some for its "difference" from the older versions, but Moffatt (like Weymouth) made it clear that his version was not intended for formal church use nor to displace the older versions.

An American Translation (1923) by Edgar Goodspeed. The purpose of this translation is admirably set forth in the preface: "For American readers, especially, who have had to depend so long upon versions made in Great Britain, there is room for a New Testament free from expressions which, however familiar in England or Scotland, are strange to American ears."

The New Testament in Modern English (1924), also known as the Centenary Translation, prepared by Helen Barrett Montgomery in commemoration of the one-hundredth anniversary of the American Baptist Publication Society.

The Revised Standard Version (New Testament, 1946; Old Testament, 1952). The copyright of the American Standard Version (1901) was held by the International Council of Religious Education, upon whose recommendation a complete revision of the 1901 version was undertaken. As in the case of the King James Version, the work was done by a committee of thirty-two scholars, divided into Old Testament and New Testament sections. On the whole, the Revised Standard Version has been well received in the English-speaking world, and a new edition—with minor changes—has been prepared by Catholic scholars.

Again, like the King James Version, it has not escaped criticism, both from those who thought it to be too liberal and others who judged it to be too conservative. One is reminded also of the attacks made on the versions of Luther and Tyndale. In addition to certain perfectly valid criticisms of textual preferences and English style, not a few personal attacks have been made on the integrity of the translators. On this point F. F. Bruce has this comment to make:

> The committee of revisers which worked on the RSV was sufficiently broadly based to make it unlikely that the version would promote any particular or sectional interest. And in fact it has found widespread acceptance in the years since its appearance in a great variety of Chris-

tian communities, theologically conservative as well as theologically liberal.[33]

The New Testament in Modern Speech (Gospels, 1952; whole New Testament, 1958). This translation by J. B. Phillips is based on the following principles:

1. The language used must be that commonly spoken.
2. The translation should expand, if necessary, to preserve the original meaning.
3. The letters should read like letters, not theological treatises.
4. The translation should "flow."
5. The value of the version should lie in its easy-to-read quality.

Its great popularity, especially among young people, has amply demonstrated the validity of these principles and the great skill of the author.

The New English Bible (New Testament, 1961). In 1947 a committee was appointed composed of representatives of the established churches of England and Scotland, the Free Churches in Great Britain, and of the Oxford and Cambridge Presses to prepare an entirely new translation of the Bible, including the Apocrypha. The general director was the brilliant British scholar C. H. Dodd, and a new Greek text was prepared under the editorship of R. V. G. Tasker. The principles by which the committee worked are stated in the introduction as follows:

> The Joint Committee which promoted and controlled the enterprise decided at the outset that what was now needed was not another revision of the Authorized Version but a genuinely new translation, in which an attempt would be made consistently to use the idiom of contemporary English to convey the meaning of the Greek. The older translators, on the whole, considered that fidelity to the original demanded that they should reproduce, as far as possible, characteristic features of the language in which it was written, such as the syntactical order of words, the structure and division of sentences, and even such irregularities of grammar as were indeed natural enough to authors writing in the easy idiom of popular Hellenistic Greek, but less natural when turned into English. The present translators were enjoined to replace Greek constructions and idioms by those of contemporary English.[34]

Reactions to this new version have been mixed, as might have been expected. Some have been repulsed by what they believe to be not only an inelegant style but positive irreverence. Others have enthusiastically accepted it as the most understandable version yet produced. Most who read it, however, find a stimulation and freshness which must have been characteristic of the original New Testament writings.

But the work must go on. The end of translations has not yet come, nor will it ever come this side of heaven, for the Word must be read and understood. So long as the world continues to change and language develops, so long as new discoveries are made and more illumination comes from the Holy Spirit, the Bible must be retranslated in order that its eternal message may always be clearly understood.

Note: A number of new versions have been published in recent years in the ongoing effort to accurately render the Bible into contemporary English. Among them are: Good News Bible, *the Bible in Today's English Version (American Bible Society, 1966, 1971, 1976);* The Holy Bible, *New International Version (Zondervan Bible Publishers, 1978);* The Jerusalem Bible *(Doubleday & Company, Inc., 1966, 1967, 1968); and* The Living Bible, *paraphrased (Tyndale House Publishers, 1971). Most recently, the New Revised Standard Version (Division of Christian Education of the National Council of the Churches of Christ in the U.S.A., 1990) has been produced by a diverse, ecumenical team of scholars. Like previous translators, this group has drawn on current understandings of biblical languages and ancient texts in its endeavor to translate original manuscripts as literally as possible into modern, understandable English.*

- What influence did Tyndale's version have on the King James Version?
- How was the King James Version made? Why was it not a translation?
- How can we evaluate new translations of the Bible?
- How can Christians help others understand the Bible today?
- If a copy of the Catholic edition of the Revised Standard

Version is available, read the introduction and discuss the changes that have been made.

Why do new translations of the Bible need to be made? Why are they frequently opposed?

Additional Resources

Beegle, Dewey M., *God's Word into English.* rev. ed. Grand Rapids, Mich.: Wm. B. Eerdmans Pub. Co., 1964.

Bruce, Frederick F., *The Books and the Parchments.* rev. ed. Westwood, N. J.: Fleming H. Revell Co., 1950.

Bruce, Frederick F., *The English Bible: A History of Translations.* New York: Oxford University Press, 1961.

Bruce, Frederick F., *History of the Bible in English.* New York: Oxford University Press, 1978.

Goodspeed, Edgar J., *The Formation of the New Testament.* Chicago: University of Chicago Press, 1925.

NOTES

1. R. O. P. Taylor, *The Groundwork of the Gospels* (London: Blackwell, 1946), pp. 25, 26.

2. George Kent, "Happily Ever After with the Brothers Grimm," *Reader's Digest,* January 1965, p. 168.

3. Archibald M. Hunter, *Introducing the New Testament,* rev. ed. (Philadelphia: The Westminster Press, 1958), p. 93.

4. Clement of Rome, *To the Corinthians,* vol. VI.

5. Hunter, *op. cit.,* p. 121.

6 Frederick F. Bruce, *Commentary on Ephesians and Colossians* (Grand Rapids, Mich.: Wm. B. Eerdmans Pub., Co., 1957), p. 166.

7. See William M. Ramsay, *Cities and Bishoprics of Phrygia,* vol. II (London: Oxford University Press, 1897), pp. 637ff., 649ff., 673ff.

8. Avery Dulles, *Apologetics and the Biblical Christ* (Westminster, Md.: Newman Press, 1963), p. 34.

9. R. V. G. Tasker, *The Nature and Purpose of the Gospels,* rev. ed., (Richmond: John Knox Press, 1962), p. 35.

10. William Barclay, *Epistle to the Hebrews* (Nashville: Abingdon Press, 1965), p. 11.

11. Jerome, *Letter to Dardanus,* 129.3; written about A.D. 414.

12. Frederick F. Bruce, *Commentary on the Epistle to the Hebrews* (Grand Rapids, Mich.: Wm. B. Eerdmans Pub. Co., 1964), p. xlii.

13. Spicq, C., *L'Epitre aux Hebreaux,* Paris, 1952, vol. 1, pp. 220-252.

14. See Richard Heard, *An Introduction to the New Testament* (New York: Harper & Row, Inc., 1951), pp. 171-172.

15. Martin Luther, *Discourses on the Fourth Gospel,* 1.5, edited by I. D. Maurice, 1867.

16. Alan Richardson, *The Gospel According to St. John* (New York: The Macmillan Co., 1962), p. 27.

17. Hunter, *op. cit.,* p. 62.

18. Edward E. Ellis, *The World of St. John* (Nashville: Abingdon Press, 1965), p. 16.

19. Charles H. Dodd, *The Johannine Epistles* (New York: Harper & Row, Inc., 1946).

20. Martin Kiddle, *Revelation* (New York: Harper & Row, Inc., 1940), p. 34.

21. Samuel A. Cartledge, *The Bible: God's Word to Man* (Philadelphia: The Westminster Press, 1961), p. 50. Copyright © 1961, W. L. Jenkins. Used by permission.

22. Alexander Souter, *The Text and Canon of the New Testament,* 2nd ed., rev. by C. S. C. Williams (Naperville, Ill.: Alec R. Allenson, Inc., 1954), p. 156.

23. Frederick F. Bruce, *The Books and the Parchments* (Westwood, N.J.: Fleming H. Revell Co., 1950), p. 108.

24. Bernard Ramm, *Special Revelation and the Word of God* (Grand Rapids, Mich.: Wm. B. Eerdmans Pub. Co., 1961), p. 180. Used by permission.

25. B. M. Metzger, *The Text of the New Testament* (New York: Oxford University Press, 1964), p. 39. Used by permission.

26. *Ibid.,* p. 86.

27. *Ibid.,* p. 195.

28. B. F. Westcott and F. J. A. Hort, eds., *The New Testament in the Original Greek* (New York: Harper & Row, Inc., 1882), p. 2.

29. *Ibid.*

30. Frederick F. Bruce, *The English Bible: A History of Translations* (New York: Oxford University Press, 1961).

31. H. W. Robinson, ed., *The Bible in Its Ancient and English Versions* (New York: Oxford University Press, 1940), p. 160.

32. Frederick C. Grant, *Translating the Bible* (New York: Seabury Press, Inc., 1961), p. 72.

33. Bruce, *The English Bible,* p. 199. Used by permission.

34. *The New English Bible: New Testament* (New York: The Oxford University Press, The Cambridge University Press, 1961), pp. viii, ix. Used by permission.